THE GOOD NEWS ABOUT JESUS

The Gospel of Mark

James M. Beaty

Seymour Press

The Good News about Jesus: The Gospel of Mark

© **James M. Beaty 2024**

All Rights Reserved. No part of the book may be reproduced in any form without written permission from Seymour Press.

© Seymour Press
Lanham, Maryland

ISBN: 978-1-938373-83-1
LCCN: 2024932783

Table of Content

Dedication i

Note to my Son ii

Foreword iii

Preface v

A Short Introduction 1

Outline of the Gospel 19

Chapter 1 25

Chapter 2 35

Chapter 3 41

Chapter 4 47

Chapter 5 55

Chapter 6 63

Chapter 7 72

Chapter 8 78

Chapter 9 88

Chapter 10 97

Chapter 11 107

Chapter 12 115

Chapter 13 124

Chapter 14 130

Chapter 15 144

Chapter 16 153

About the Author 161

Dedication

With Faith, Hope, and Love,
to

My son, Mark Ulrich Beaty

My daughter-in-law, Jamie Charlene Pitre Beaty

My grandson, Isaiah James Beaty
&
My granddaughter, Carmen Camille Beaty

A Note to my Son

Dear Mark,

When you were in kindergarten, you made a bookmarker for your mother, who loved you very much. It was a piece of yarn thread; on one end, tied to a paper candle that you had made and colored. On the other end, it was tied to an open book (representing the Bible), on which was written: Matt 5.16:

> Live your life in such a way,
> So that others may see your good works,
> And give glory to your Father,
> Who is in Heaven! (JMB)

🕯 📖 🕯

There is a parallel between natural things and spiritual things. Just as we need natural light to be able to see and read, we need the light of the Holy Spirit to help us see what God's Word says and t understand it. We should always seek to make sure that God is the King of our lives and that we are in loving and grateful obedience to what He commands us to do. The Words of the Gospel will always bless you.

Lots of Love,

Dad

Foreword

It has been a privilege to have known Dr. James M. Beaty since January 1973, when I found myself in a mini-term New Testament Survey course at Lee College in Cleveland, TN. As I recall, the course was offered as an opportunity for students to catch up or get ahead in their studies, as it was required for graduation. Amazingly, hundreds of students registered for the course as Dr. Beaty, with a cadre of senior-level undergraduates, gamely sought to introduce this multitude to the history and content of the New Testament. Even then, his conviction about the role of orality in the interpretation of these texts was evident, since part of the course involved a component of listening to the reading of the New Testament corpus.

This conviction was formed through experiences such as being part of the Pentecostal tradition, where the orality of worship services involves many auditory prompts and cues, his extensive missionary activity in a variety of cultures and languages, and his advanced training in New Testament at Vanderbilt University where he became the first Pentecostal to acquire a Doctor of Philosophy degree in Biblical Studies. His approach to the biblical text has been field-tested in numerous graduate seminars devoted to 1 Corinthians and Acts, at the Pentecostal Theological Seminary, where he served as the Academic Dean and Professor of New Testament for over twenty years.

This volume is the fruit of a lifetime of preparation and reflection on the biblical text in the context of the believing community. It comes from one whose intellectual acuity remains sharp well into his nineties, and is a testament to a lifelong dedication to enriching the spirituality of the everyday believer and local church. In it, readers will find a fresh approach to an ancient and familiar text that has sometimes been submerged by interpretive agendas that obscure, rather than illuminate, its beauty, practicality, and timeliness.

In a brief introduction, Beaty exposes the reader to some of the reception history surrounding this Gospel and seeks to place the new reading or hearing in an expansive interpretive context. Next, his extensive outline of the Gospel highlights the important turns the reader can expect in this new reading. Finally, Beaty employs his multi-linguistic gift to introduce us to a unique presentation that comes from a deep love of the story the text seeks to convey.

I congratulate my teacher, colleague, and friend for offering this work to a broad audience and commend it as a helpful instrument for gaining new insight into Mark's Gospel. May it find its target.

Dr. John Christopher Thomas,
Clarence J. Abbott Professor of Biblical Studies
Pentecostal Theological Seminary
Cleveland, Tennessee USA

Preface

I did not start out to translate the Gospel of Mark. Rather, I first intended to update the King James Version for my son, Mark. So, I downloaded it and used my knowledge from coursework in Biblical Studies and my ability to speaks English, Spanish, French and Haitian Creole, but who has also studied Hebrew, Greek, Latin, and German, and my experience in living in Latin America for sixteen years, that caused me to do a lot of oral translating.

A Short Introduction to The Gospel of Mark

Who wrote the Gospel of Mark?

In seeking an honest answer, the procedure must be: (1) Ask the right questions focused on the needed information and (2) Look at the text and the multifaceted aspects of the context.

But, first, what do we know for sure? There are two things no one can doubt: (1) The name of the author of the Gospel is not given within the Greek text of the document, and (2) only the Greek title, "Kata Markon" ("According to Mark"), is attached to all copies of the text that have survived from antiquity.

Catholic scholar Brant Pitre [1] affirms that:

> (1) The first and perhaps biggest problem for the theory of the anonymous Gospels is that no anonymous copies of Matthew, Mark, Luke, or John have been found. As far as we know, they do not exist, and never have.
> (2) When it comes to the titles of the Gospels, not only the earliest and best manuscripts, but all ancient manuscripts— without exception, in every language— attribute the four Gospels to Matthew, Mark, Luke, and John.
> (3) There is "absolute uniformity" regarding the authorship of each book.

---

[1] Brant Pitre is Distinguished Research Professor of Scripture at the Augustine Institute Graduate School. He earned his Ph.D. in Theology from the University of Notre Dame, where he specialized in the study of the New Testament and ancient Judaism (From his biography - online).

(4) The oldest Greek copy of the beginning of the Gospel starts with the title "The Gospel according to Mark" (Greek: <u>Euangelion kata Markon</u>)."[2]

So "Mark" (whoever he was) wrote the book. But the question that remains is "Which Mark is he?"

Was Mark One of the Twelve Apostles?

The answer must be "No!' because his name does not appear on any of the four lists of the Apostles (not even the one he produced.) The four lists are in Matthew, Mark, Luke, and Acts. (There is no list in John).

If not an Apostle, Where did Mark get His Information?

Many people were present at some point in the ministry of Jesus and could speak of one or two miracles He performed. But no one, except an Apostle, or someone from the small group that traveled with Jesus (including a few men[3] and the women who provided food), would have seen all that Jesus did. So, what connection did Mark have to any of the apostles?

First, Mark's home in Jerusalem was the primary meeting place of the first Christians, including the Apostles. It is generally referred to as the "House of Mary, the mother of John (from his Hebrew heritage) or Mark (from his cultural

---

[2] Brent Pitre, *The Case for Jesus. The Biblical and Historical Evidence for Christ* (Image, 2016), Online.

[3] Cf Acts 1.15-26. The person elected to replace to Judas Iscariot was such a person.

heritage)." Therefore, Mark would have had access to all that was known about Jesus, including His ministry, death, and resurrection.

From both New Testament and outside sources, we learn that Peter and Mark worked together in Rome near the end of their lives.
- (1) In his first letter around A.D. 62/63, Peter wrote that the church" here" sends you greetings, and so does my son, Mark" (5.13).
- (2) Papias, who lived from about 60 to 130 A.D. and, for part of that time, was Bishop of Hieropolis (in modern Turkey), wrote that Mark was especially helpful to Peter in Rome and, on one occasion, serve as the translator while Peter ministered to a group of Roman soldiers Army, that asked Mark to write down those beautiful things, in a beneficial [4] form.

So When and Where Did the Peter and Mark's Paths Cross?

Simon bar-Jonah (Peter) and his brother, Andrew, along with their father, Jonah, ran a family fishing enterprise in the village of Capernaum, on the northwest corner of the Sea of Galilee. Near them was the Zebedee family fishing enterprise with the two sons, James and John. And there must have been many other such businesses, because products from the Sea of Galilee, such as dried tilapia, salted sardines, and Garum

---

[4] Papias used the Greek word *Creia* (Pronunciation: "CRAY-ah" like CRAY-on). This is my English transliteration of the Greek word that is used. Two recent books on the form are: Hock, Ronald F. and Edward N. O'Neil, *The Chreia in Ancient Rhetoric* 1, (1986), Atlanta: Scholars Press and Vol. 2, 2002, Atlanta: Society of Biblical Literature).

(a fermented fish sauce) were highly esteemed, even in parts of Europe. There were fifteen ports from which products could be shipped from Capernaum to areas around the Sea of Galilee. Further, shipments to Europe or North Africa could be made from Haifa on the Mediterranean.

After his Bar-Mitzvah, there were three annual feast days on which every male Je was mandated by the Mosaic Law to come to the Temple in Jerusalem. So, three times each year, there were two reasons to visit Jerusalem—one was religious and the other commercial.[5]

Galilee and Jerusalem are separated by nearly a week's walk. And it is possible that well before he became a follower of Jesus, Peter was in contact with Mark's family. In fact Andrew and Simon became followers of Jesus while in Judea (Andrew heard John the Baptist proclaim that Jesus was the Lamb of God, so he found Simon and took him to Jesus.[6] (And later, Peter may have been the one who led Mark's mother to faith in Jesus. And we know that all of these were in Jerusalem together in the same house in the week that Jesus died, and apparently, many times later.

---

[5] A hint of the commercial aspect of their visits to Jerusalem is that John is well known in the palace of the high Priest (it was like "Hey! This is the man who brings our fish from Galilee."). Also, Jesus had selected "Peter, James, and John" to be with Him on special occasions. What should that be called?" A leadership committee? ❖ By the time of Agrippa (twelve years after the crucifixion), Peter had moved out to the surrounding areas of Judea and James was overseeing the work in Jerusalem. So in Acts, when Agrippa I (to gain favor from the Jews) decided to blot out the leadership of the new movement, he grabbed James, immediately beheaded him, and went looking for Peter and arrested him. But it was too near the feast to execute him, and he decided to wait. So the Lord delivered Peter. Since John was the third ranking leader (and, therefore, next on Agrippa's list), it became necessary for both Peter and him to remove themselves from the immediate reach of King Agrippa.

[6] John 1:4-42).

Tradition says Mark and Peter's families were related, through either Peter or his wife. But since we have no credible source or form of the tradition, I assume the strong relationship between Peter and Mark was spiritual. Peter's reference to "my son, Mark"[7] probably refers (1) to the fact that Peter led Mark to accept Jesus as his Lord and (2) guided his early growth in Christ. Remember that "sonship" has to do with birth and growing up.

Since Mark's mother's house was the location of the Last Supper and where the 120 tarried and prayed until the Day of Pentecost, it became the "main" meeting place of the church in Jerusalem.

Peter was deeply involved with work in the Jerusalem church and the surrounding areas[8] and from that early period, "the ends of the earth" loomed ahead as a challenge. So he must have had a formative influence on Mark's early Christian life. And from the beginning of their acquaintance, he must have recognized that Mark, with his bi-cultural and linguistic gifts could also be helpful to him (and others) in ministry to any group that did not speak Aramaic.

The unanimous tradition from the early church is that Mark based his Gospel on the teaching of Peter. Mark is affirmed to have written this gospel by such early church Fathers as Papias, Irenaeus, Justin Martyr, Clement of Alexandria, Eusebius, and Tertullian, as well as by the Muratorian Fragment and the Anti-Marcionite Prologues.

---

[7] 1 Peter 5:13
[8] See Acts 1-12

In his article, *Mark, the Evangelist, His African Memory*[9] William H. Oliver, professor of the Philosophy, Practical and Systematic Theology, at the University of South Africa, Pretoria, summaries the life of Mark as seen by Thomas Oden (*How Africa shaped the Christian mind* [2007] and *The African memory of Mark* [2011].[10]

The history handed down by the church in Africa (i.e., especially in Alexandria), is that either Mark's parents or grandparents had moved to the area of Libya and lived there for some time, before or near the time that Jesus was born. But as seen in the New Testament, they were one of the many families who had returned to the homeland and were known as "the Hellenists"[11] because they used Koine Greek and had been influenced by aspects of Greek culture.

The family had bought a large, comfortable home near the Temple. This home is referred to by Luke as the house of "Mary, the mother of John, also called Mark."[12] This reflects the family's bi-cultural nature since "John" comes from Hebrew/Aramaic ("Yohanan") and "Mark" comes from Latin ("Marcus"). So he should be referred to as "John/Mark" (like Saul/Paul), i.e., "John" in the Jewish world and "Mark" in the Roman world, though the Bible never refers to him as "John Mark".

---

[9] Willem Oliver, "Mark the Evangelist: His African Memory" HTS Theological Studies, 72:4 (2016) http://dx. doi.org/10.4102/ hts.v72i4.3400.

[10] See section "An Exposition of the Life of Mark," in this article.

[11] Cf. Acts 6:1.

[12] Acts 12:12.

Mark's father is not identified in the New Testament. Within the tradition, however, his name is "Aristopolos" or "Arostalis. It is said he was converted when he and Mark were on a journey in the Jordan Valley when a lion and a lioness approached them. The father told Mark to escape for his life, while he faced the lions. But as Mark began to pray and rebuke the lions they dropped dead.

Tradition has it that Mark's mother continued to live in Jerusalem, until her death in A.D. 58.[13]

The Coptic Church presents an article on the contribution of Mark to the church in Africa.[14]

St. Mark the Apostle, [15]
The Founder of the Coptic Church

The Coptic Church[16] or the Church of Alexandria is called "The See of St. Mark"; one of the earliest four sees: Jerusalem, Antioch, Alexandria, and Rome.

St. Mark, the Founder

The Copts are proud of the apostolicity of their Church, whose founder is St. Mark; one of the seventy Apostles (Mk

---

[13] "Saint Mary, the Mother of Mark (First Century) Catholicism.org," https://catholicism.org/saint-mary-the-mother-of-mark-first-century.html#:~: text=Saint%20Mary%20was%20the%20mother,Apostles%20at%20the%20first%20Pentecost.

[14] The Administration of the Orthodox Coptic Church in the Southern United States gave permission to edit the article on from their website. It is slightly revised it and some footnotes have been added.

[15] "Apostle" means "One who is sent." Mark was not one of the Twelve Apostles of Jesus, but one of those "called by the lord and sent by the church."

[16] The word, *Coptic*, derives from an old form of the word *Egypt*. The *Coptic* language is an ancient form of *Egyptian* (not Arabic).

10:10),[17] and one of the four Evangelists. He is regarded by the Coptic hierarchy as the first of their unbroken 117 patriarchs, and the first of a stream of Egyptian martyrs.

This apostolicity was not only furnished on grounds of its foundation but rather by the persistence of the Church in observing the same faith received by the Apostle and his successors, the Holy Fathers.

St. Mark's Biography

St. Mark was an African native of Jewish parents who belonged to the tribe of Levi. His family lived in Cyrenaica until they were attacked by some barbarians and lost their property. Consequently, they moved to Jerusalem with their child John/Mark (Acts 12:12, 25; 15:37).

Apparently, he was given a good education and became conversant in both Greek and Latin in addition to Hebrew and Aramaic. His family was highly religious and in close relationship with the Lord Jesus Christ. His cousin was St. Barnabas and his father's cousin was St. Peter.[18] His mother, Mary, played an important part in the early days of the Church in Jerusalem. Her upper room became the first Christian church in the world where the Lord Jesus Christ Himself instituted the Holy Eucharist (Mk 14:12-26). Also, this is the same place where the Lord appeared to the disciples after His resurrection and His Holy Spirit came upon them.

---

[17] The mission of the seventy is mentioned in the New Testament, but the names of the seventy are never mentioned. And no specific person is identified as being one of the seventy.

[18] In the New Testament this is not recorded, but there are hints of close affiliation between Peter and that family.

Young Mark was always associated with the Lord, who chooses him as one of the seventy. He is mentioned in the Holy Scriptures in several events related with the Lord. For example, he was present at the wedding of Cana of Galilee and was the man who had been carrying the jar when the two disciples went to prepare a place for the celebration of the Passover (Mk 14:13-14; Lk 22:11).

St. Mark and the Lion

The voice of the lion is the symbol of St. Mark for two reasons: (1) He begins his Holy Gospel by describing John the Baptist as a lion roaring in the desert (Mk 1:3). And (2) His famous story with a lion, as related to us by Severus Ebn-El-Mokafa: Once a lion and lioness appeared to Mark and his father, Arostalis, while they were traveling in Jordan. The father was very scared and begged his son to escape, while he awaited his fate. Mark assured his father that Jesus Christ would save them and began to pray. The two beasts fell dead and because of this miracle, his father believed in Christ.

Preaching with the Apostles

At first, St. Mark accompanied St. Peter on his missionary journeys in Jerusalem and Judea. Then he accompanied St. Paul and St. Barnabas on their first missionary journey to Antioch, Cyprus and Asia Minor, but for some reason or another he left them and returned home (Acts 13:13).

On their second trip, St. Paul refused to take him along because he left them on the previous mission; for this reason St. Barnabas was separated from St. Paul and went to Cyprus with his cousin St. Mark (Acts 15:36-41). There, he departed in the Lord and St. Mark buried him.[19] Afterwards, St. Paul needed St. Mark, and both preached in Colosse (Col 4:10), Rome (Phil 24; 2 Tim 4:11) and perhaps in Venice.

In Africa

St. Mark's labor in Africa was the high point of his ministry. When he left Rome, he went to Pentapolis,[20] where he was born. After planting the seeds of faith and performing many miracles he traveled to Egypt, through the Oasis, the desert of Libya, Upper Egypt and then entered Alexandria from its eastern gate in 61 A.D.

On his arrival, the leather strap on his sandal had become loose. So he went to a cobbler to have it mended. When the cobbler, named Anianos took an awl to work on it, he accidentally pierced his hand and cried out in a loud voice "O One God." At this utterance, St. Mark rejoiced and after miraculously healing the man's wound, took courage and began to preach to the hungry ears of his convert.

The spark was ignited and Anianos took the Apostle home with him. And he and his family were baptized, and many others followed.

The spread of Christianity must have been quite remarkable because pagans were furious and went out seeking for St. Mark everywhere. But being aware of the danger, the Apostle ordained a bishop (Anianos), three priests and seven deacons to look after the congregation if anything should happen to him.

---

[19] This was handed down by the Church,
[20] Pentapolis (literally, five cities) was in northern Africa.

So he left Alexandria and went to Berce, and then on to Rome, where he met St. Peter and St. Paul and remained there until their martyrdom in 64 A.D. On returning to Alexandria in 65 AD, St. Mark found his people firm in faith and thus decided to visit Pentapolis. There, he spent two years preaching and performing miracles, ordaining bishops and priests, and winning more converts.

Finally he returned to Alexandria and was overjoyed to find that Christians had multiplied so much that they were able to build a large church building in Baucalis,[21] at the edge of the city.

His Martyrdom

In the year 68 AD, Easter fell on the same day as the Serapis feast.[22] The furious heathen mob had gathered in the Temple of Serapis in Alexandria and then descended on the Christians who were celebrating the Glorious Resurrection at Baucalis. St. Mark was seized, dragged with a rope through the main streets of the city, while the crowds were shouting "The ox must be led to Baucalis," a precipitous place full of rock where they fed the oxen that were used in the sacrifice to idols. When night came the saint was thrown into prison, where he was cheered by the vision of an angel, who strengthened him by saying, "Your hour has now come, Dear Mark, the good minister, to receive your recompense. Be encouraged, because your name is written in the book of life." When the angel

---

[21] "Baucalis" means (roughly), 'the cow pasture.'

[22] In Greek mythology, Serapis (pronounced seh-RAH-pis and sometimes spelled Sarapis) had been a god of the underworld. But Ptolemy I Soter (reign: 305–284 B.C.) remodeled him as the deity of the sun and introduced him to Egypt, with the center of the cult in Alexandria. Little by little Serapis was entreated for healing and problems of fertility.

disappeared, St. Mark thanked God for sending His angel to him. Suddenly, the Savior Himself appeared and said to him, "Peace is with you, Mark; you are my disciple and my evangelist!" St. Mark started to shout, "O My Lord Jesus!" But the vision disappeared.

On the following morning probably during the triumphal procession of Serapis he was again dragged around the city until he was dead. The flesh of his body was torn and bloody, and it was their intention to cremate his remains, but the wind blew, and the rain fell in torrents and the people dispersed. Then the Christians secretly took his body and buried him in a grave that they had carved out of the rock under the altar of the church.

His Apostolic Acts

St. Mark was a broad-minded Apostle. His ministry was quite productive and covered a large field of activities. These include:

1. Preaching in Egypt, Pentapolis, Judea, Asia Minor, and Italy during which time he ordained bishops, priests, and deacons.
2. Establishing the "School of Alexandria" which defended Christianity against philosophical school of Alexandria, which produced many great Fathers.
3. Writing the Divine Liturgy of the Holy Eucharist which was modified later by St. Cyril to the Divine Liturgy known today as the Divine Liturgy of St. Cyril

-oOo-
The Four-Line Format

The translation of the Gospel of Mark presented here is formatted in the oral tradition of four lines, called a "Tetra-Colon," ("tetra" means "four" and "colon: means "line"). In antiquity, all reading was oral reading. Yes! You heard me correctly. There was no such thing as silent reading in antiquity!

This format grew out of, and was molded by, the process of speaking and writing. That was a world where most people could not read or write. A written communication (letter, etc.) had two focal points: (1) Origination and (2) Delivery. At the point of origination, the sender of the communication dictates the message to a scribe, who puts it into written form. And at delivery, it would be read out loud to those to whom it was addressed (i.e., it goes from written form back to oral). The pattern is (1) from oral to written and form, and then (2) from written to oral form. This served as an alternative to the sender making a visit and being present with the group that is addressed.

We can easily overlook the physical process of speaking, both at the point of origin and delivery. As we know, spoken words are produced by forcing air (breathe/spirit) through the voice box (larynx), where the vocal cords vibrate according to mental stimulation. Air, forced from the lungs, produces words and phrases.

As a bellows, the size of the lungs is a limiting factor in speaking, because the air that goes out must be replaced to continue speaking. And our system of grammatical punctuation reflects that function, e.g., the period ["."] (which used to be called the "full stop"), the comma [","] (which used to be called the "short-stop"), and the colon [:] /semi-colon [;] (which used to be called the "half-stop." The old terms refer to the amount of time one stops speaking to renew their air supply. At the same time, these breaks became an oral device to help people understand and memorize the text.[23]

Oral culture functioned differently from modern culture in many ways. I my earlier ministry, my wife and I spent several years in Haiti start a training school. We lived in Haiti where 85% of the people were illiterate. The former missionaries left a Jamaican cook to work for us. And since she spoke English, my wife, Virginia, made a list of eighteen or twenty items that we needed from the market, and started to hand it to Frances, who said to her, "Madame, I can't read!" That was a culture shock for Virginia. So she said, "What are we going to do?" But Frances replied, "No problem, Ma'me! Just tell me what you want." So Virginia read the list to her and gave her the money, Frances thought she would need. On returning home, she had bought every item on the list, told my wife how much she paid for each item, and gave her the correct chain. That is a shocker for most moderns! Further, there are thousands of Christians across Haiti who are illiterate but who can sing every verse of several hundred hymns and spiritual songs from memory.

-o0o-

When I started updating the KJV I put my update into what I call "sense lines," as I had done in my teaching of 1 Corinthians in Seminary. I soon saw that several verses fell

---

[23] Form Britannica (online).

into four lines and that all the text could be formatted in the same way.

In the classical Greek and Latin prosody[24] or "patterns of rhythm and sound used in poetry," the Encyclopedia Britannica defines the "tetracolon" (tetra means four; and colon means line) as "a period made up of four colons (JMB: lines)"

So, I concluded that this is the form and structure of the Gospel of Mark. But marvel of marvels, it is also the Word of God, or as Mark, himself, states it, it is "The GOOD-NEWS about Jesus, who is both the Messiah and God's Son!"[25]

The four-line structure of prose appears to me to have a direct relationship to the four-line hymns of Ambrose in the fourth century. During the 4th-century A.D., when Ambrose, the famous bishop of Milan, hymn singing was already common in the East, having begun among heretics. Ambrose introduced both hymn singing and a new type of chanting, the Western Church from that became known as the Ambrosian Chant.

Matthew Britt points out that although the earliest poetry did not rhyme or have a fixed number of syllables, it may have had certain poetic features like parallelism. [26] For him, all speech has what rhythm could be called "natural rhythm." He

---

[24] Pronunciation: PROS-oh-dee.
[25] The SBL Greek New Testament omits "Son of God," but the internal text of Mark supports its inclusion.
[26] Matthew Britt, *The Hymns of the Breviary and Missal* (New York: Benziger Brothers, 1924), pp. 25-32 on 'meters.'

sees this "rhythmical" pattern illustrated in the Song of Moses.

> I will **sing** to the **LORD**,
> For **He** is **highly** ex**al**ted.
> > The **horse** and its **rider**
> > He **hurled** into the **sea**.
>
> The **LORD** is my **strength** and my **song**;
> He has **become** my **salvation**.
> > **He** is my **God**, and I will **praise** him,
> > My **father's** God, and **I** will **exalt** him.[27]

It can also be seen in my oral formatting of John 3:16:

> For **God** so **loved** the **world**,
> That He **gave** His **One** and Only **Son**,
> > So that **whoever** *believe*s in **Him**,
> > Should not **perish**, but **have** eternal **life**.

Britt says that what he calls the "quantitative principle' in poetry was developed by the Greeks and passed to the Romans in the second century B.C. This divided the short (weak) and long (strong) syllables and arranged them in patterns called "feet" in various combinations.

Meter

There are strong and weak syllables in spoken prose or poetry. A weak syllable followed by a strong syllable is called an "iamb" (eye-AM) or an iambic (eye-AM-bic) foot. A metron has two feet. Any sentence formed of iambs is in

---

[27] (Exodus 15:1f).

iambic meter. A foot of two strong syllables is called a spondee.

Forms of Iambic Meter

If the rhythm is based on feet (as in the most modern poetry), it is called the "Iambic Tetrameter" ("tetre" = four), but if it is based on the "metron," as Britt does, it is called "Iambic Dimeter" as in "Be-FORE the END - ing OF the DAY." for example. We call such rhythm "Long Meter" (88.88).

Considering all this, and to get the most out of the text, it text should be read (1) out loud, and (2) slowly, but (3) with the mind in gear, even when one is reading to oneself!

May God bless those who read and hear this Good News! Amen!

James M. Beaty
January 30, 2024

Outline of The Gospel of Mark

Part I
(Chapters 1-9)
The Good News about Jesus, As Foretold by the Prophets, Especially by the Prophet Isaiah
(1:1)

I. Prelude - 1:2-13

A. John: The Messenger (1:2-8)
  1. The Prophecy about John (1:2-4)
  2. John: Preaching and Baptizing (1:5-8)

B. Jesus: the Messiah (1:9-13)
  1. The Baptism of Jesus by John (1:9-11)
  2. The Testing of Messiah (1:12-13)

II. The Ministry of Jesus - 1:14-6:29

A. The Early Galilean Ministry (1:14-3:12)
  1. The Heart of His Message (1:14-15)
  2. Recruiting the Twelve **(1:16-20)**
     a. Simon and Andrew (1:16-18)
     b. James and John (1:19-20)

B. One Sabbath in Capernaum (1:21-34)
  1. Surprised by His Teaching (1:21-22)
  2. Healing a Demoniac (1:21-29)
  3. Healing Simon's Mother-in-law (1:30-31)
  4. Healing & Casting out Demons (1:32-34)

C: The Preaching Mission in Galilee (1:35-45)
    1. It Starts with Prayer (1:35-39)
    2. Healing a Leper (1:40-45)
D: Conflict with the Religious Leaders (2:1-3:6)
    1. On Forgiving Sins (2:1-12)
    2. On Mingling with Sinners (2:13-17)
    a. Calling of Levi (2:13-14)
    b. Dining with Levi (2:15-17)
    3. On Fasting (2:18-20)
    a. Old Garments (2:21)
    b. Old Wineskins (2:22)
    4. On the Sabbath and…
       a. Work (2:23-28)
       b. Healing (3:1-6)
E: Summation of Early Ministry (3:7-19a)
    1: Healing and Deliverance for Many 3:7-12
    2: Ordaining the Twelve Apostles 3:13-19a

III. Opposition increases in Galilee

A. Rejection and Opposition (3:19b-22)
    1. By His Friends in Capernaum (3:19b-21)
    2. By the Scribes (3:22)
B. And His answer (3:23-35)
    1. To the Scribes
       (Sin vs Holy Spirit) 3:23-30
    2. To His Family Outside 3:31
       To His Spiritual Family: Inside 3:32-35
C. How the Word is Received (4:1-34)
    1. The Sower Sows the Seed
       a. Why He Uses Parables (4:1-8)
       b. An Explanation of the Parable (4:13-20)
    2. Openness: Nothing can be Hidden (4:21-23)

  3. Teaching on 'How Seeds Grow'(4:26-29)
D. Authority and Power (4:35-6:4)
  1, Calming the Sea of Galilee (4:35-41)
  2, Healing a Demon-possessed Man (5:1-20)
  3, More Miracles in Galilee (5:21-43)
 4. Unbelief in Nazareth (6:1–6)
E. Six Teams 'to preach and to heal" (6:7–13)
 And King Herod's Reaction (6:14–29)

IV. Beyond Galilee (6.30-9:29

A. To the East of the Sea of Galilee (6:30-52)
B. To the West of the Sea of Galilee (6:53-7:23)
C. To Syro-Phoenicia (7:24-30)
D. To the Region of the Decapolis (7:31-8:10)

V. Closure of His Ministry in Galilee (8:11-38)

A. Who is Jesus? Peter answers.
 1. The Confession of Peter:
  "You are the Messiah!" 8:11-31
 2. The Teaching of Jesus
  "On His Death and Resurrection" (8:32-38)
 3. And Peter's Rebuke/Correction8:31-33
 4. Jesus: On Discipleship (8:34-38)
B. Who is Jesus? God answers.
 The Climax of the Revelation (8:31-9:50)
 1. The Transfiguration (8:31- 9:29
 2. And the Departure from Galilee (9:30-50)

Part II
Chapters 10-16)

I. Ministry in Judea and Beyond Jordan (10:1-52)
   A. Teaching concerning the Family (10:1-16)
      1. Concerning Divorce (10:17-12)0
      2. Concerning Children (10:13-16)
   B. The Rich Young Man (10:17-31)
   C. A Request of Two Brothers (10:32-45)

II: The Last Week/Passion Week: 10:40-15:47
   A. Sunday (11:1-11)
      1. Healing of Bartimaeus (10:46-52)
      2. The Royal Entry (11:1-10)
      3. A Short Visit (11:11)

   B. Monday (11:12-19)
      1. Cursing the Fig Tree (11:12-14)
      2. Clearing the Temple (11:15–19)

   C. Tuesday (11:20-13:37)
      1. The Fig Tree and Faith (11:20-26)
      2. Jesus and the Jewish Leaders (11:20-12:44)
         a. His Authority Questioned (11:27-33)
         b. The Wicked Vineyard Keeper (12:1-12)
         c. Questions:
            1) Paying Tax to Caesar (12:13-17)
            2) On the Resurrection (12:18-27)
            3) The Greatest of the Commandments (12:28-34)
            4) The Question of Jesus: David's Son (12:35-37)
      3. Jesus and His Disciples (12:38-13:27)
         a. Beware of the Scribes (12:38-44)
   b. Signs of the End (13:1-37)

D. Wednesday (14:1-11)
1. Authorities plotting to Kill Jesus (14:1-2)
2. The Anointing of Jesus in Bethany (14:3-9)
   3. Judas Made the Deal (14:10-11)

E. Thursday (14:12-16)
1. Thursday: Two Disciples sent
      To prepare the room (for two nights)
      With instructions (14:-11)
 2. Thursday Night (already Jewish Friday):
    a: The Last Supper (14:12-26)
    b: Prayer in Gethsemane (14:26-42)
    3. The Arrest in the Garden (14:43-52)

F. Friday (14:53-15:47)
   1. Trial before the High Priest 14:53-65
      And Peter's Denial (14:66-72)
   2. Trial before Pilate (15:1-14)
      And the Flogging (15:1-15)
   3. Mockery in the praetorian
      And March to Calvary   15:16-23
   4. Crucifixion,
      And Mockery
   5. Mark's two Witnesses at the Cross:
      a. The Centurion (Gentile) (15:24-39)
      b. The Women, (Jewish) (15:40-47)

G. Saturday: In the Tomb

H. Sunday (16:1-11)
   1. The Three Women at the Tomb   (16.1-8)
   2. First Appearance to Mary Magdalene (16:9-11)

III. Conclusion (16:12-20)
    A. Later Appearances (16:12-18)
    1. To Two Disciples (16:12-13)
       2. To the Eleven [With Signs] (16:14-18)
    B. Jesus and the Apostles (16:19-20)
      1. Jesus Ascends (16:19)
       2. The Apostles start the Mission (16:120)

CHAPTER 1

ಸಿ 📖 ಣ [28]

The Prophecy About
The Messiah and the Messenger

1. (1:1-2a)

This is the beginning of the Good News
About Jesus, the Messiah and the Son of God,
    As it was foretold by the prophets
    And described in more detail by Isaiah.[29]

2. (1:2b)

And remember this![30]
"I am sending my Messenger,
    And he will go before you,
    To prepare the way for You."[31]

3. (1:3)

He will roar like a lion,
As he proclaims his message in the desert:
    "Prepare the Way of the Lord!
    And make the path before Him smooth!"

---

[28] I have used the "Rose" and the "Book" as "markers" to remind us of the Living Word" (Jesus) and the Written Word.

[29] See footnotes of SBL Greek text. Mark sees Jesus as the Servant of God that is pre-announced in Isaiah 40-66, and who, based on chapter 53, is called the "Suffering Servant." So "Messiah has come!" is the "beginning of the Good News about Jesus."

[30] Exodus 23:20 (Malachi 3.1); the next verse is from Isaiah 40.3.

[31] The word "behold" (KJV) is *idou* in Greek; it is the second person-singular imperative of the verb, to "look at," to "see" (i.e., to "understand") and results in knowing. It is an "attention–grabber," like the English: "Hey! Look! This is important!"

The Coming of the Messenger

4. (1:4)

One day John, the Baptizer[32] showed up in the desert.
And this is what he was proclaiming to the people!
  "In order to be forgiven of your sins,
  You must repent[33] and be baptized!"

5. (1:5)

And large crowds came out to hear him,
From all parts of Judea, and even from Jerusalem;
  And after they confessed their sins,
  John baptized them in the Jordan River.

6. (1:6-7a)

John's clothing was made of camel's hair[34],
And he used a strip of leather as a belt;
  His diet was locusts and wild honey,
  And this is the message that he preached.

---

[32] John, a priest by birth and a prophet by calling, was sent by God to tell the people to turn to God (faith) from sin (repentance) because Messiah was coming. And, where possible, one was to make amends (restitution) for the wrong(s) that they had done. And only then could one be baptized. But many people were offended, saying that John was treating the Jews like Gentiles. Proselyte baptism was developed in the inter-testamental period. It was based on turning from sin (and making amends for wrongs done) and turning to God to serve and obey Him; it involved complete immersion of oneself and by oneself), (under the direction of a rabbi). ❖ John was preaching and baptizing on the east side of the Jordan River, a little over twenty (20) miles from Jerusalem.

[33] The Hebrew word for "repent" is shouve ('to turn' to God from sin.) Therefore, this turning includes both repentance and faith. Thus it is NOT: "Come, be baptized and that will result in forgiveness of sins!" BUT "Turn to God from sin" and (that will result the forgiveness of sins) and then, come and be baptized as witness to what God has done for you and as a pledge and a public witness of one's loyalty to God.

[34] Also referred to as "sack cloth."

7. (1:7b-8)
"Someone, greater than I am, is about to appear,
And I am not worthy to untie His sandals.
   I have been baptizing you in water,
   But He will baptize in the Holy Spirit."

෨ 📖 ෬
The Baptism of Jesus
8. (1:9-10a)
In those days Jesus of Nazareth came from Galilee,[35]
And He was baptized in the Jordan River by John;
   As Jesus was coming up out of the water,
   He saw the heavens, as it were, split open.
9. (1:10b-11)
And the Spirit descended on Him like a dove;
And a voice from heaven said,
   "You are my Beloved Son;[36]
   I am well pleased with You."[37]

෨ 📖 ෬
The Testing of the Messiah
10. (1:12-13)
Then, at once, the Spirit led Him out into the desert.
Where He was tested for forty days by Satan.
   Yes! He was there among the wild animals,
   But angels came and served him.

---

[35] That was about 70 miles.
[36] See Psalm 2:7, About Messiah as King.
[37] See Isaiah 42.1, About Messiah as Priest.

The Early Ministry of Jesus in Galilee
11. (1:14)
After the arrest of John,
Jesus returned to Galilee,
> Where He began to proclaim
> The Good News about God's Kingdom.

12. (1:15)
"The long-awaited time," He said, "has now arrived,
And the Kingdom of God has drawn near;
> So, turn from your sin and rebellion
> And put your trust in the good news from God."

Recruiting the Twelve:

-o0o-
Simon and Andrew
13. (1:16)
One day as Jesus was walking by the Sea of Galilee,
He saw Simon…and Andrew, his brother;
> They were casting a net into the sea,
> Because that was what they did for a living.[38]

14. (1:17-18)
And Jesus says to them, "Hey! Come with me!
And I will teach you how to fish for men!"
> So they left their nets,
> And followed Jesus.

---

[38] We know from the Gospel of John that Simon and Andrew were, at first, disciples of John the Baptizer, and that Andrew, after hearing John say, "Hey! Look! That is the Lamb of God…" went and bought Simon (his brother) to Jesus (John 1:35-42). But after John was put in prison, both went back to their fishing in Galilee. Here Jesus invites them to be trained with Him, which means that they will be full-time, with Jesus, in training or ministry, from that point on.

-oOo-
James and John

15. (1:19)

Then, as Jesus walked on a little further,
He saw James, the Son of Zebedee,[39]
    And John, his brother;
    They were sitting in a boat…mending their nets.

16. (1:20)

And as soon as Jesus called them,
They left their father, Zebedee,
    In the boat, with the hired help,[40]
    And they went with Jesus.[41]

---

[39] There were no "family names" at that time and a man was known as the "son" of his father. When the sons of Zebedee are mentioned, James is always mentioned first and would appear to be older. When Agrippa I became king of Judea (AD 41), he attempted to find favor with the people by slowing the rapid growth of the Christian faith. He beheaded James, and arrested Peter, planning to execute him, after Passover.

[40] The Zebedee Fishing Company was more than a parallel to a family garden. It had hired employees and was a functioning unit in the national economy.

[41] The Jonah family (the family of Peter (Simon, son of Jonah) and the family of Zebedee and Salome (parents of James and John) appear to be closely related in business and may have operated as one: The Galilean Fish Company. Peter and James, the older brothers, apparently represented the authority of the respective families, but John appears to have been involved in deliveries to Jerusalem and was therefore known in the house of the High Priest. Peter, James and John appear as a group with Jesus on several occasions (as if in training). For example, they are with Him at the transfiguration, when he goes to pray, or inside a private home to heal a person. Later, the three appear to be the "executive committee" in the early day after the ascension.

☙ 📖 ❧
One Sabbath in Capernaum
17. (1:21-22)
Then Jesus, with His disciples, went to Capernaum,
And on the Sabbath[42] He taught in the synagogue;
   And they were amazed at His authority in teaching,
   Because the scribes did not teach with authority.[43]

☙ ❁ ❧
The Witness of an Evil Spirit
18. (1:23)
Then one day, a man, who was demon possessed;
Attended the synagogue;
   And suddenly the evil spirit cried out,
   Saying, "Leave us alone, Jesus of Nazareth!
19. (1:24)
"Does what we do bother you?
Have you come to destroy us?
   I know who you are!...
   You are the Holy One from God!"
20. (1:25-26)
Then Jesus rebuked him, saying,
"Do not speak, but come out of him!"
   And the evil spirit threw the man down,
   Cried with a loud voice, and came out of him.

---

[42] This is the first Sabbath story of conflict. In the first century the synagogue was much more open to public comment than the modern Protestant church. ❖ The scribes taught by citing earlier teachers, sometimes, one "for" and another "against" the subject. But when Jesus taught, He said, "But I say to you…"

21. (1:27)
And they were all absolutely amazed; and…
They began to say to each other, over and over again,
"What is this? A new teaching with authority!
Look! Even the evil spirits obey Him!"
22. (1:28)
And the news about what Jesus had done,
Began to spread rapidly;
And it went out, by word-of-mouth,
Over the nearby region of Galilee.

ಸಾ ❀ ಆ
Healing Simon's Mother-in-law
23. (1:29-30)
When the service was over, Jesus, James and John
Went home with Simon and Andrew;
And they found that Simon's mother-in-law
Was sick and in bed with a fever.
24. (1:31)
So they go to where she is resting,
And Jesus takes her hand and lifts her up;
And, at that very moment, the fever leaves her,
And she begins to serve them.

☙ ❀ ❧
Many Healed After Sunset

26. (1:32-33)

That evening, after sunset,
The people began to bring to Jesus
    All the sick and demon-possessed;[44]
    And the whole village gathered outside the door.

26. (1:34)

And Jesus healed many, with all kinds of diseases;
And He cast out many demons;
    But He did not let the demons speak,
    Because they knew Him.[45]

☙ 📖 ❧
A Preaching Mission across Galilee

27. (1:35)

Then early the next morning,[46]
While it was still dark,
    Jesus gets up and goes out to a solitary place,
    Where He begins to pray.

28. (1:36-37)

Later, Simon, and others who followed Jesus,
Come out, looking for Him.
    And when they find Him, they say,
    "Hey! Everybody is looking for You!"

---

[44] A Jew could do no work on the Sabbath, but the Sabbath ended at sunset; so after sunset they could bring their sick ones to Jesus.

[45] This is an indirect witness to who Jesus is.

[46] The Roman term "morning" was used for the fourth watch of the night (3:00-6:00 AM).

29. (1:38)
But Jesus replied and said,
"Let us go on to the next villages,
   So that I may do what I came to do, i.e.,
   To proclaim the Good News there also!
30. (1:39)
So, Jesus began to travel and to minister
Over all the region of Galilee,
   Preaching in their synagogues
   And casting out demons.

- oOo -

The Healing a Leper

31. (1:40)
One day a man with leprosy came to Jesus:
He fell down on his knees before Him
   And pleaded with Him earnestly, saying,
   "Sir, if you choose to do so, you can heal me."
32. (1:41)
So Jesus, since He was moved with compassion,
Reaches out His hand to him,
   And as He touches him, He says, "Yes!
   That is what I choose to do! Be healed!"
33. (1:42-43)
And at that moment, the leprosy disappears;
And he was completely healed.
   And Jesus, speaking sternly to him,
   Sent him away at once, with these instructions.

34. (1:44)
"Make sure that you say nothing to anyone
But go directly and show yourself to the priest;
    And offer, as a testimony to them,
        What Moses commanded for your healing."

-oOo-
Impact: Pressure on Jesus
35. (1:45a)
But the man, who was healed of the leprosy,
Left and began to spread the news everywhere;
    And then, the news, about his healing,
        Continued to spread by word-of-mouth.

36. (1:45b)
And this kept Jesus from entering the town openly,
So He remained out-of-sight, on the outskirts,
    And people came from everywhere,
        Looking for Him.

CHAPTER 2

Conflict
With the Religious Authorities
About the Forgiveness of Sins

37. (2:1-2)
A few days after Jesus got back to Capernaun,[47]
It became known that He had returned;
    And so many people came, looking for Him,
    That there was no room for them, even at the door.

38. (2:3)
While Jesus was inside the house,
Teaching the Word to those who had come,
    The friends of a paralyzed man
    Brought him to Jesus, to be healed.

39. (2:4a)
But they could not even get close to Jesus
Because there were so many people there;
    So they uncovered a part of the roof
    Where Jesus was sitting.

---

[47] Capernaum was his "hometown" and He lived (I think) with Peter (in the home place of his father, Jonah, who shared the name of the reluctant prophet, Jonah (in the Old Testament) who had lived in Gat ("wine press"), a town that is mentioned in Joshua 10.13 and 2 Kings 14.25). The ruins of Gat are located just over 3 miles north of Nazareth. One might wonder if Jonah, the father of Peter, had been named for the prophet or was it possible that they were distant kin?
❖ The house of Jonah (the father of Peter and Andrew) in Capernaum was a large, modest house in its day (See the article by the Staff of Biblical Archeology Society. entitled, "The House of Peter: The Home of Jesus in Capernaum?" (Online). And the climate was dry and sub-tropical, because it was located 682.14 feet below sea level ❖ Easy access to the flat roof was provided by an outside stairway against a wall and The flat roof, itself, consisted of long beams, covered by hand-hewn planks, laid across the beams, and covered with mats made of organic fiber, covered with dirt that was well pressed down.

40. (2:4b-5)
Then they lowered the lame man on his pallet.[48]
And, when Jesus saw their faith,
    He says to the lame man, "My son,
        You have been forgiven of your sins."

41. (2:6-7)
And this caused some of the scribes, sitting there,
 To think, "Why does this man say that?
    What a blasphemy!
        Because no one, but God, can forgive sins!"

42. (2:8)
Bur, knowing immediately what they were thinking
And the question that was bothering them;
    Jesus says to them,
        "Why do you focus only on that?

43. (2:9)
"Is it easier to say to the lame man,
'Your sins are forgiven!'
    Or to say to him,
        'Get up! Pick up your pallet and walk!?'

44. (2:10-11)
"But…So that you may know that the Son of Man
Has authority on earth to forgive sins"…
    Jesus says to the lame man, "I say to you,
        Get up! Pick up your pallet and go home!'"

45. (2:12)
So he got up, picked up his pallet and left at once,
As everyone looked on, with sheer amazement;
    And the people began to praise God by saying,
        "We have never seen anything like this before!"

---

೫೦ 📖 ೦೩
The Calling of Levi
46. (2:13-14a)
One day, as Jesus was walking along the beach;
A large crowd gathered, and He taught them.
    And as He was moving on from there,
    He saw Levi bar Alphaeus.[49]

47. (2:14b)
Levi was sitting at a table, collecting taxes;[50]
But when Jesus said to him,
    "Follow me,"
    Levi got up and followed Jesus.

-o0o-
Dining with Levi
48. (2:15)
Later, while Jesus was dining at Levi's house,
Many of the tax collectors and sinners
    Were seated with Jesus and his disciples,
    Because they also had begun to follow Jesus.

---

[49] "Matthew" is the name that Mark uses in his list of the Twelve (3:18). He was a priest; from one of the 24 groups of the tribe of Levi, which served in the temple, one week at a time, twice each year. The rest of time they did secular work.

[50] He was collecting taxes for Rome, of course; and that made him a despised figure, plus, as agents of Rome, they often collected more than was due. Some of the different kinds of taxes collected by the Roman authorities at that time were: "a. salt tax, b. crown tax, c. grain tax (one-third of the produce), d. tax on fruit and nut trees (one-half the produce), e. poll tax, f. tithe, g. tribute and h. imposts/duties" (cf K. C. Hanson, "The Galilean Fishing Economy and the Jesus Tradition" (Online).

49. (2:16)
But, when the Scribes and the Pharisees
Saw Jesus eating with tax-collectors and sinners,
   They said to his disciples, "Why does Jesus
   Eat with tax-collectors and sinners?"

50. (2:17)
When Jesus heard it, He says to them,
"Those who are sick need to see a doctor;
   But those, who are healthy, do not!
   I came to call sinners, not the just."

෨ 📖 ଓ
Fasting: The Old vs the New:

51. (2:18)
John's disciples and the Pharisees were fasting
 And someone came and asked Jesus,
   "Why do they fast?
   But your disciples do not fast?"[51]

52. (2:19a)
And Jesus said to them,
"Is it possible
   For the wedding party to fast,
   While the bridegroom is still with them?

---

[51] Jewish Encyclopedia: "Fast and Fast Days":
   All Jewish fasts begin at sunrise and end with the appearance of the first stars of the evening, except those of the Day of Atonement and the Ninth of Ab, which last "from even till even."
And Jewish Virtual Library-Jewish Holidays: Fasting and Fast Days:
   It was customary to hold public fast days on Mondays and Thursdays (Tosef. to Ta'an. 2:4)… On some occasions, the fast was not a total one, but people refrained only from meat, wine, anointment with oil, and other pleasures.

53. (2:19b-20)
No! While the bridegroom is with them,
They cannot fast.
> But after the bridegroom is taken away,
> That is the time, when they will fast.[52]

ഔ 📖 ൟ
The Old Garment
54. (2:21)
No one puts a patch of new cloth on an old garment,
Because the new patch will shrink when washed,
> And it will tear away from the old garment,
> And the result is: the tear is then worse than it was.

-oOo-
The Old Wineskins
55. (2:22)
And no one stores new wine in old wineskins:
Because the new wine will burst the old wineskins
> And both will be lost;
> So, new wine needs to go into new wineskins.

ഔ ✤ ൟ
About Work on the Sabbath
56. (2:23)
One Sabbath, Jesus was walking through a wheat field;
And His disciples, as they were going through it,
> Began to break off
> Some of the heads of wheat.

---

[52] According to the Didache (8:1), an early Christian document about doing missionary work among the Gentiles, the church has shifted the fast days to Wednesdays and Fridays (and that is why we have prayer-meetings on Wednesday nights and, also, why Catholics eat fish on Friday, each week.)

57. (2:24)

And one of the Pharisees said to Him,
"Look, why are they doing
   What is not permitted to be done
   On the Sabbath?"

58. (2:25)

And Jesus says to them,
"Did you never read about what David did,
   When he and those who were with him
   Were in need and hungry?

59. (2:26)

"He went into God's House and ate the "Holy Bread,"
When Abiathar[53] was the high priest.
   Yet the Law, only allows the priests to eat of it,
   But David even gave it to those with him!"

60. (2:27-28)

Then Jesus said to them,
"The Sabbath was made for man (generic);
   And man was not made for the Sabbath:
      Thus the Son of Man[54] is also Lord of the Sabbath."

---

[53] (1) As the leader of the Exodus, Moses took upon himself the role as the very first priest (something like, High Priest), and Aaron, with his sons Nadab, Abihu, Eleazar, and Ithamar, served as priests in the tabernacle. (2) In the latter period of the Judges (after Israel entered Canaan), the descendants of Ithamar, Aaron's fourth son, carried out the duties of the high priest. (3) In the time of King David, there were two priests: Ithamar's descendant Abiathar (Pronunciation: ah-BUY-uh-THAR) and Eleazar's descendant Zadok. After Abiathar joined David's son Adonijah, in his treason against David, Abiathar was removed from the office of priest according to King Solomon. Since then, the descendants of Zadok, from the line of Eleazar, are the ones that have served as high priest

[54] Jesus often used the phrase "the Son of Man" to refer to Himself. But there is long history in the Old Testament of this phrase being used as a synonym for "man" (in the generic), cf Psalm 8:5 (JMB)
   What is man that You are mindful of him,
   And the son of man that You care for him?

CHAPTER 3

About Healing on the Sabbath

61. (3:1)

On another Sabbath Jesus
Went to the synagogue;
    And there was a man there
    Whose had was paralyzed.

62. (3:2)

And the people watched Jesus closely,
To see if He would heal the man
    On the Sabbath,
    So that they could accuse Him.

63. (3.3)

Then Jesus said
To the afflicted man,
    "Hey! Stand up!
    Here in the middle!"

64. (3:4a)

Then Jesus said to them,
"Is it lawful, on the Sabbath,
    To do good or to do evil?
    To save life or to take it?"

65. (3:4b-5a)

Then all of them became completely silent.
And Jesus looked around at them, with anger.
    But there was a deep sadness in His heart,
    Because of the hardness of their hearts.

And the meaning here is probably that, although He is fully human, He still has divine authority.

66. (3:5b)

So He said to the man,
"Lift up your hand!"
   And the man lifted his hand;
   And it became normal, like his other hand.

The Pharisees Leave: to Plot
67. (3:6)

And, as a result, the Pharisees got up and left;
They went immediately to consult with the Herodians
   About how they might join forces
   In order to destroy Jesus.[55]

-o0o-
But Jesus Leaves: to Serve
68. (3:7a)

Then Jesus and His disciples
Also got up and left;
   But they went down by the waterfront;
   Where many Galileans had come to see Jesus.

-o0o-
Healing and Delivering Many
69. (3:7b-8)

And there were many people there
From Judea and Jerusalem.
   And many more from Idumea and Trans-Jordan;
   And even from around Tyre and Sidon.

---

[55] Note how early it was in His life that the opposition to Him reached such a point that his opponents began to seek for a way to destroy Him.

70. (3:9)

And He told His disciples
To have a small boat, ready, and on stand-by,
   So that if the crowds pressed on Him too hard,
   He would have a way of escape.

71 (3:10)

Because, since He had healed so many,
All that were sick or afflicted
   Pushed hard to get close to Him,
   Because everybody wanted to touch Him.

72. (3:11-12)

And when the unclean spirits saw Him,
They fell down before Him, and cried out,
   "You are the Son of God!"
   But He sternly ordered them not to make it known.

72. (3.14-15)

And He ordained the following twelve,
So that, they might be with Him
   And be sent out to preach
   And to have authority to cast out demons.

73. (3.16-17)

And He chose: Simon,
Whom He re-named, 'Peter';
   James, son of Zebedee, and John, his brother;
   Whom He re-named "The Sons of Thunder!"

74. (3.18-19a)

And also, Andrew, Philip, and Bartholomew,
Matthew, Thomas, and James, son of Alphaeus,[56]
   With Thaddaeus and Simon, from Cana,
   And Judas Iscariot, who betrayed Him.

---

[56] If Matthew and James are sons of Alphaeus, what about Thomas?

The Rejection of Jesus
By His Friends

75. (3:19b-20)

Then they went back to Capernaum;
And a large crowd gathered around the house;
   It was so large that Jesus and His disciples
   Had no time, not even to eat. [21]

76. (3:21)

And when His family heard about this,
They came to rescue Him:
   Because they said,
   "He needs some rest!"[57]

77. (3:22)

But the scribes who came from Jerusalem said,
"No! That's not it! He's possessed by Beelzebub![58]
   And He casts out demons
   By the prince of the demons!"

78. (3:23)

Then Jesus invited the scribes to come closer
And He began to teach them,
   By exposing their own logic,
   That "Satan could cast out Satan.'

79. (3:24-25)

"If a kingdom is divided against itself," He said,
"That kingdom cannot stand;
   And, if a house is divided against itself,
   That house cannot stand.

---

[57] To be "beside oneself" is to be out of control emotionally, to be hysterical, insane, mad, overwrought, or upset.

[58] Pronunciation: bee-EL-zee-BUB.

80. (3:26)
"And if Satan should rise up against himself,
And thus become divided,
    Then he cannot stand,
    But he will defeat himself.

81. (3:27)
No one can enter the house of a strong man
And take from him what belongs to him,
    Unless the strong man is first defeated and tied up;
    Then one can take what belongs to him.

-oOo-
Warning: Sin against the Holy Spirit

82. (3:28)
Listen! Because what I am telling you
Is absolutely true;
    Any sin that a person commits may be forgiven,
    Even the sin of cursing God.

83. (3:29-30)
"But whoever speaks evil of the Holy Spirit
Has no forgiveness, in this world or the next."
    And Jesus said this…because they had said,
    "He has an evil spirit."

-oOo-
His Family: Biological vs Spiritual

84. (3:31)
Then His mother and His brothers came;
And standing outside, at the edge of the crowd,
    They sent a verbal message to Him,
    Asking to see Him.[59]

---

[59] This is an example of one of the many aspects of oral culture that surprise and shock us. We might write a note, ask that it be passed on to the speaker, and hope; but they were certain that their oral message would be delivered.

85. (3:32)

And soon, someone sitting near Him,
Says to him,
   "Hey! Your mom and Your brothers are outside;
   And they want to see you."

86. (3:33-34)

But Jesus says, as He glances around about Him,
"My mother and my brothers! Who are they?"
   And then He says, "Whoever does the will of God…
     <u>That</u> is my brother, my sister and my mother.

CHAPTER 4

The Sower Sows the Seed

87. (4:1a)
One day, as Jesus began to teach by the seaside,
A large crowd, as usual, gathered around Him;
    So He climbed into a boat, that was there,
    And He sat down to teach them.

88. (4:1b-2)
And all the people stood on the beach,
Right up to the edge of the water.
    And He used many comparisons[60] in His teaching,
    And one of them was the following.

89. (4:3-4)
"Learn from this! A man went out to sow seed.[61]
And as he was sowing,
    Some of the seed fell on the hard, compacted path,
    And the birds flew down and ate it.

90. (4:5)
"And some of it fell in a place, with solid rock,
Very near the surface:
    And almost immediately, it sprouted;
    But it had very little soil to nourish it

---

[60] I have used the English word, "comparison" (to compare one thing to another) for the word "parable" (Greek: pah-rah-bow-LAY, which mean "placed beside," i.e., to illustrate. Most of what we know as parables are stories, but the New Testament also uses the word for other types of comparisons that Jesus made.

[61] "To sow seed" is to scatter seed. "To plant" seed is to find a place, open a hole, insert the seed and cover it. Wheat and barley seeds are scattered.

91. (4:6)

"So, when the sun came up,
It was scorched immediately;
   And since it had no root,
   It withered and dried up.

92. (4:7)

"And some of the seed fell among thorns,
And when the thorns grew up,
   They choked it;
   So that part of the seed bore no fruit at all.

93. (4:8)

"But most of the seed fell on good ground,
Where it sprouted and grew,
   And when it reached maturity, it produced…
   Thirty, sixty or a hundred times what was sown. [9]

94. (4:9-10)

And then He said,
"Let anyone, who has ears to hear, hear!"[62]
   But when alone, the twelve and those with him[63]
   Asked Him about the comparisons He had used.

---

[62] "Hear" has two meanings: (1) to hear in a physical sense and (2) to hear and understand and to heed (or to obey).

[63] The Group that traveled with Jesus consisted of:
(1) the Twelve,
(2) a small group of men described in Acts 1:21f as:
(Young's Literal)
T]he men who did go with us during all the time
in which the Lord Jesus went in and went out among us, beginning from the baptism of John, unto the day in which he was received up from us…and
(3) a larger group of women of means and status, apparently managed by Mary Magdalene, who had been touched and greatly blessed by the ministry of Jesus and consequently wished to be near Him and to learn from Him and, at the same time, to facilitate and be a part of what He had come to earth to do.

95. (4:11)
And He replied, "The secret of God's kingdom
Has been given to you;
> But, for those on the outside, everything
> Is given in comparisons and symbols.

96. (4:12a)
"Consequently, when they look, they think they see,
But they do not grasp the meaning;
> And when they listen, they think they hear,
> But they do not heed.

97. (4:12b)
"And thus, they do not understand,[64]
Because, if they did understand,
> Their lives would be changed,
> And they would be forgiven of their sins."[65]

98. (4:13)
And then He says to them,
"Do you not understand this comparison?
> And if that is the case,
> How will you understand the other comparisons?

-o0o-

The Interpretation

99. (4:14-15a)
"The sower was sowing the Word.[66]
And the hard path on which the seed fell,
> As the Word was being sown,
> Is a person that is not fully receptive.

---

[64] What they do not understand is this: the Messiah must first suffer and that later He would set up the physical kingdom

[65] Note: the need of the work of the Holy Spirit to convict and to draw to Christ.

[66] That is, "God's Word" or "The Good-News about Jesus."

100. (4:15b)
"Thus, after hearing the Word,
Satan comes at once
    And takes away the Word
    That was sown in their hearts.

101. (4:16)
"And some of the seed fell
On a thin layer of earth covering stone;
    They hear the Word and receive it with joy;
    But they have no soil to nourish their roots.

102. (4:17)
"And without a good root system,
They only endure for a short time;
    And when affliction or persecution comes,
    Because of the Word, they soon turn back.

103. (4:18)
"And then, there were the seed
That fell among the thorns;
    These are those
    Who hear the Word.

104. (4:19)
"But…the cares of this world,
The desire for wealth and other things
    Come in and choke the Word,
    So they *never* bear fruit.

105. (4:20)
"But the seed that fell on good ground…are those
Who, when they hear the Word, they embrace it,
    And these bring forth fruit…
    Thirty, sixty, and a hundred times what was sown.

Openness: Nothing can be Hidden

106. (4:21)

Then He says to them, "When you light a candle,
 You do not put it under a basket or a bed, do you?
  No! When you light a candle,
  You put in on a candlestick.

107. (4:22)

"Because there is nothing secret,
That will not be revealed;
 And there is nothing concealed,
 That will not be exposed."

108. (4:23f)

And He says to them, "If you have ears to hear
Take heed and obey the Word;
 Pay attention to what you hear…Because
 The measure you give is the measure you get!

109. (4:25)

"To the person, who already has,
More shall be given;
 But from the one who does not have,
 Even what he has shall be taken away."

110. (4:26-27a)

Then He said, "God's Kingdom is like this:
A sower sows seed on the ground;
 And then he sleeps, but he gets up
  And checks on it, every night and every day.

111. (4:27b-28a)

"So whether he sleeps or whether he watches,
The seeds sprout and grow:
    Without the sower knowing[67] how;
    Because the earth, by itself, produces the harvest.

112. (4:28b)

"First, there is the stalk and the blade of the plant,
Then, the undeveloped heads of wheat,
    And finally, the full grains of wheat reach maturity.
    Within the heads of wheat.

113. (4:29)

"And, as soon as the grain is ripe,
The sower begins to gather it in,
    Because the time of the harvest
    Has come."

The Story of the Mustard Seed

114. (4:30-31a)

And He said, "How can we compare God's Kingdom?
And what comparison shall we use to compare it?
    It is like a mustard seed,
    The smallest of all the seeds, sown in our fields.

115 (4:31b-32)

But once the seed is sown, it grows up,
And becomes the largest of all our shrubs,
    And it produces large branches, so that
        The birds of the air build their nests in its shade.

---

[67] Who programmed the DNA of the seed?

-oOo-
The Teaching Method of Jesus
116. (4:33-34)

Jesus spoke the Word to them, with many comparisons,
As they were able to understand it.
    And He did not speak to them, without a parable
    But, alone with His disciples, He explained it all.

ಬ ❀ ಚ
The Calming of the Wind and the Waves
117. (4:35-36)

After sunset that day, Jesus says to his disciples,
"Let us go over to the other side of the lake!"
    And so, after He had let the people go,
    They took Him, just as He was, into the boat.

118. (4:36bf)

And there were other boats that followed them.
But soon…a strong windstorm came up,
    And the waves began to break over into the boat
    And the boat began to fill up with water.

119. (4:37af)

But Jesus continued to sleep
On a pillow in the back of the boat;
    So they wake Him up
    And they say to Him,

120. (4:38bf)

"Master, do you not care
That we are about to perish?"
    So He wakes up,
    And rebukes the wind.

121. (4:39b)

Then He said to the sea, "Stop![68] Be still!"
And, at that very moment,
    The wind stopped blowing;
    And there was a great calm.

122. (4:40a)

So He says to them,
"Why are you so fearful?
    Do you not put
    Your trust in God?"

123. (4:40bf)

He said this because they were paralyzed with fear,
And then they began to say to each other,
    "Wow! Who is this?
    Even the wind and the sea obey Him?"

---

[68] The Greek text has "Peace" (Shalom) the Jewish word of greeting. One dimension of peace is the calming down of motion and agitation. It could also be translated, "Welcome! Calm down!" There was a "welcome" because sail boats need wind to move them.

CHAPTER 5

The Gentile Demoniac

124. (5:1f)
When they got to the other side of the sea,
To the country of the Gerasenes,[69]
    A demoniac from the cemetery confronted Jesus,
    Just as Jesus got off the boat.

125. (5:3)
The man lived in the caves
Where the people in that area buried their dead;[70]
    And no one could bind him,
    Not even with chains.

126. (5:4)
Because he had been bound many times,
And frequently, he had been tied down with a chain;
    But he had always broken the chains
    And he always escaped from the shackles.

127. (5:4f)
No one had the strength to control him.
So, both in the tombs and in the mountains, nearby,
    He was always making a lot of noise
    And cutting himself with stones, day and night,

---

[69] The country or area of the Gerasenes (GEH-rah-SEENS): Mark and Luke refer to the area of the Gerasenes, while Matthew uses the term, Gadarenes (GAH-dah-REENS). This area is southeast of the Sea of Galilee. And there was an ancient village called Gadara (gah-DAH-rah) in this area. Most of the inhabitants were non-Jewish.

[70] In those days last rites for the dead included being anointed with spices and oils (to reduce the smell as the body decays), wrapped tightly in a large linen cloth and laid in a cave. When the flesh is consumed, the bones are placed in a bone-box, which is labeled and stored, often in the same tomb.

128. (5:6fa)

But when he saw Jesus,
Even at a distance,
    He ran and bowed down before Him;
    And, in a loud voice, he says,

129. (5:7b)

"Jesus, Son of the Most High God,
Why are you coming here, where I am?[71]
    I beg You, in the name of God,
    Do not torment me!"

130. (5:8af)

Because Jesus had just said to him,
"Come out of him, you evil spirit!"
    Then Jesus asked him,
    "What is your name?"

131. (5:9bf)

And the evil spirit said to Jesus,
"My name is Legion, because we are many."
    And he begged Him earnestly
    Not to send them into exile.

132. (5:11f)

At the same time there was a large mass of hogs,
Rooting and eating on a hill nearby.
    And the evil spirits begged Jesus, saying,
    "Allow us to go into the hogs!"

133. (5:13a)

And Jesus gave them permission
To do just that;
    And when the demons went out of him,
    They entered the hogs.

---

[71] Or "What have I to do with You?"

134. (5:13b)

And the entire herd,
Consisting of about two thousand hogs,
    Ran down the steep incline into the sea,
    And they were drowned in the water.

135. (5:14a)

Then the hired help ran away
And began to tell what had happened,
    To everybody, both in the town
    And in the surrounding countryside.

136. (5:14b)

And that caused
A lot of people to come out,
    To see for themselves
    What had happened.

137. (5:15)

And when they came to where Jesus was,
They saw the man, who had been possessed;
    He was sitting there, clothed, and in his right mind.
    And they were seized with fear.

138. (5:16f)

Then the eyewitnesses began to tell those arriving,
About what had happened to the man, and to the hogs.
    And the people began to beg Jesus
    To go away …and to leave them alone.

139. (5:18b-19a)

And as Jesus was getting into the boat,
The man, who had been delivered,
    Asked if he could go with Jesus.
    But Jesus said, "No!

140. (5:19b)
"Go back home to your family and to your friends,
And tell them what great things
    The Lord has done for you,
    And how He has had mercy on you."

141. (5:20)
So the man left… and, in that area of Decapolis,
He began to proclaim,
    What great things Jesus had done for him;
    And all the people were amazed.

ഇ ❦ ര

Stories of Faith and Disbelief:
The Faith of Jairus

142. (5:21)
Then Jesus went back to the other side of the Sea;
And as soon as He arrived,
    A large crowd of people gathered around him,
    Almost as soon as He got off the boat.

143. (5:22fa)
Then an elder, named Jairus, from the local synagogue,
Came, looking for Jesus
    And, when he saw Him, he fell down before Him,
    And began to plead earnestly with Him, saying.

144. (5:23b)
"Sir! My daughter is at the point of death;
Would You, please, come,
    And lay Your hands on her,
    So that she may be healed and live."

-oOo-
The Woman Who Touched Jesus
145. (5:24f)
And as Jesus was leaving to go with Jairus,
A lot of people, eager to be near Him, followed;
    Among these, there was a woman,
    Who had had a bleeding problem for twelve years.
146. (5:26)
She had suffered greatly and seen many doctors.
And although she had spent everything that she had,
    Still, she had not improved,
    But on the contrary, she was getting worse.
147. (5:27)
So, when she heard about Jesus,
She joined in with the crowd,
    And as she came up behind Him
    She touched His garment.
148. (5:28f)
Because she had said,
"If I can only touch His clothes, I shall be healed!"
    And immediately, the bleeding had stopped;
    So she knew that she was healed of her affliction.
149. (5:30)
And Jesus, of course, was also aware, immediately,
That power had had gone out from Him.
    So He turns around in the crowd, and says,
    "Who touched my mantle?"
150. (5:31)
And His disciples say to Him,
"Master! Do You not see the crowd?
    Everybody is pushing up against you,
    And You still ask, 'Who touched me?'"

151. (5:32fa)
But after Jesus had turned around,
He saw who had touched Him.
   And the woman became afraid and was trembling,
   Because she knew what had happened to her.

152. (5:33b)
So she stepped forward
And fell down at His feet,
   And told Him exactly
   What had happened.

153. (5:34)
And Jesus says to her,
"Daughter, your faith has delivered you!
   Go in peace,
   And be healed of your affliction!"

-oOo-
Back to Jairus

154. (5:35)
And while Jesus was still speaking, servants arrived
From the house of the elder of the synagogue,
   And they say to him, "Sir, your daughter is dead!
   So…why bother the Master anymore?"

155. (5:36)
But Jesus overheard
What they were saying,
   So He said to the ruler of the synagogue,
   "Do not fear! Just trust me!"

156. (5:37)
So Jesus went on with the elder,
But He took with Him,
   Only Peter, James and John,
   The brother of James.

157. (5.38)

And when they got to the elder's house,
Jesus saw the disorder:
> There was so much weeping...
> And loud wailing!

158. (5:39a)

And when He went inside,
He says to them,
> "Why are you in such grief?
> Why are you weeping, like this?"

159. (5:39b-40a)

"The girl is not dead!
She is just asleep."
> But they just laughed at Him;
> So He sent them all outside.

160. (5:40b)

Then He took the child's father and mother,
Along with those who had come with him,
> And they went into the room
> Where the child was in bed.

161. (5:41)

And after taking the child's hand,
He says to her,
> *"Talitha cumi!"* [72]
> Which means, "Young lady, stand up."

162. (5:42)

And the little girl,
Who was twelve years old,
> Got up immediately and walked.
> And all of them were amazed.

---

[72] Pronunciation: TAH-lee-thath COO-mee

163. (5:43)

Then He told them…
To feed her,
    But He also gave them strict orders
    Not to tell anyone, about her healing.

CHAPTER 6

Disbelief and Rejection in Nazareth

164. (6:1-2a)
So Jesus left and went to Nazareth, where He grew up,
And His disciples went with Him;
   On the Sabbath they attended the synagogue
   Where He began to teach.

165. (6:2b)
Many of those who heard him were amazed and said,
"Where did this man get all this ability?
   Why is such wisdom given to him?
   How can He perform such mighty miracles?

166. (6:3)
Is this not the carpenter, the son of Mary,[73]
And the brother of Jim, Joey, Jude, and Sim[74]?
   Are not His sisters still here with us?"
   They said this because they were offended at Him.

167. (6:4)
So Jesus said to them,
"A prophet is honored everywhere,
   Except in his hometown,
   In his own family and in his own house."

168. (6:5f)
And He could do no extraordinary miracles there,
Although He healed a few sick people,
   By laying His hands on them;
   And He was amazed at their unbelief.[75]

---

[73] Mark gives no history of the birth of Jesus; but here he acknowledges that Jesus is "Mary's son. It appears that Joseph is no longer alive at this point.

[74] The diminutive or Jacob, Joseph, Jude and Simon; like "Jude" for Judas.

[75] Unbelief shuts the door!

The Mission of the Twelve

169. (6:6-7)

After that Jesus went from village to village, teaching.
And one day He called the twelve together
    And began to send them out, in groups of two,
    And He gave them authority over evil spirits. [8]

170. (6:8-9a)

And these are the instructions that He gave them,
"Take nothing for your journey, except your staff:
    No bread, no bag, no money in your belt,
    Keep your sandals on and do not wear two tunics."[76]

171. (6:10)

He also said to them,
"When you accept an invitation
    To be a guest in a home,
    Stay there until you leave that area.

172. (6:11)

"And if the people of any place refuses to welcome you
Or will not even listen to you,
    When you leave, shake off the dust from your feet
    As a witness against them." [12]

-o0o-

173. (6:12-13)

So they went and preached that all should repent:[13]
And they cast out many demons;
    They also anointed, with oil, many that were sick
    And they were healed.

---

[76] A "tunic" was a full body gown with two long sleeves.

174. (6:14a)
And soon, after that, Herod, the King,
Heard about what was going on,
    Because almost everybody was talking about
    This man named Jesus.

175. (6:14b)
And some were even saying,
"John, the Baptizer, has come back from the dead!
    And that is why
    All these miracles are being performed."

176. (6:15)
Others said, "Wow! This is Elijah!"
But others said, "No!
    He is just an ordinary prophet,
    Like those in the old days."

177. (6:16)
But when Herod heard about it,
He said, "That... is John,
    The same one that I beheaded,
    He has risen from the dead!

-oOo-

A Flashback:
On the Death of John the Baptizer

178. (6:17)
Now Herod had arrested John and put him in prison
In order to please Herodias[77],
    Whom Herod had married... in spite of the fact,
    That she was the wife of his brother, Philip.

---

[77] Pronunciation: herr-ROw-dee-US.

179. (6:18-19)
Herod had arrested John, because John had said to him,
"You have no right to marry your brother's wife."
    And that was also why Herodias
    Was so angry at John, that she wanted to kill him.

180. (6:20a)
But she could not;
Because Herod feared John,
    Sense he knew
    That John was a just and holy man.

181. (6:20b)
Therefore, Herod protected him;
And many times, he would talk with him;
    And when he did, he became perplexed, But…
    Herod was always glad to hear what John had to say.

182. (6:21)
One day, however, Herod held a banquet;
It was his birthday and he had made that day a holiday,
    So that all his high-ranking officers were there,
    As well as the top-level social class of Galilee.

183. (6:22)
And after the daughter of Herodias danced for them,
Herod and his guests were so delighted,
    That the king said to the young woman,
    "Ask whatever you will, and I will give it to you."

184. (6:23)
And he swore to her with an oath,
"Yes! Whatever you ask of me,
    I will give it to you,
    Up to half of my kingdom."

185. (6:24)
So she went and asked her mother,
"What should I ask?"
    And her mother said,
      "Ask for the head of John the Baptizer."

186. (6:25)
So she went straight back to the king and said,
"Sir, I want you to give me
    The head of John the Baptizer
    On a platter, right now."

187. (6:26-27a)
Although the king was very upset and sorry;
Yet because of his oath and his invited guests,
    He would not refuse her;
    So Herod commanded a guard to bring John's head.

188. (6:27b-28)
So the guard went, as he was commanded,
And he beheaded John in the prison;
    Then he brought his head on a platter
    And gave it to the young woman.

189. (6:28-29)
And she gave it to her mother.
And when the disciples of John heard about this,
    They came and took away his body
    And laid it in a tomb.

ൕ ❀ ଓ
After the Twelve Return

190. (6:30)
After the apostles returned from their mission,
They had a meeting with Jesus;
    And they reported to Him all that they had done
    And all that they had taught.

191. (6:31)
Then Jesus said to them, "Let us find a quiet place
And rest for a little while!"
   Because so many people were coming and going
   That they had no time---not even to eat!

-oOo-
Withdrawals from Galilee
192. (6:32fa)
Then they left in a boat,
Seeking a quiet place, in order to be alone.
   But many people saw them leave
   And they figured out what was happening.
193. (6:33b)
So they ran ahead in groups
Out of all the near-by towns
   And a lot of people got there
   Even before the boat arrived

-oOo-
Feeding the Five Thousand
194. (6:34)
So when Jesus arrived, He saw a lot of people
And He was moved with compassion for them,
   Because they were like sheep without a shepherd,
   So He began to teach them many things.
195. (6:35)
In the late afternoon that day,
His disciples come to him and say,
   "This is an isolated place
   And… it's getting late in the day.

196. (6:36)

"Send them away,
So that they may go into the countryside
 Or to some near-by village
 And find a place to buy some food."

197. (6:37)

But the answer of Jesus was,
"Why do you not give them something to eat?"
 And they say to him, "Shall we go
 And buy enough bread[78] to feed them *all*?"

198. (6:38)

And Jesus says to them,
"How many loaves do you have? Go and see!"
 And as soon as they find out, they say,
 "We have five loaves of bread and two fish!"

199. (6:39f)

Then He told the people to be seated,
In groups, on the green grass.
 And they sat down
 In groups of fifty and one hundred.

200. (6:41a)

Then, taking the five loaves and the two fish,
And looking up to Heaven,
 Jesus blessed and broke the loaves,
 And gave it to His disciples to share with the people

201. (6:41bfff)

Then He divided the two fish among them all.
And they all ate and were no longer hungry:
 Then they took up twelve baskets of left-over food;
 And there were five thousand people who ate.

---

[78] The Greek text gives "two hundred denarii" as the estimated cost, and the denarius was about a day's labor. The question is "Do they have that much money?" and the answer is, "They had partners who provided for them.?

202. (6:45f)
When His disciples had finished eating, He told them
To get into the boat and to go back to Bethsaida.
   And when He had finished sending the people away,
   He, Himself, went up on the mountainside to pray.

-oOo-
Walking on the Water
203. (6:47fa)
Late that night, while the boat was still at sea,
And Jesus was still on the mountainside,
   He saw them in distress, rowing the boat,
   Because a strong wind was against them.

204. (6:48b)
And, then, about three o'clock in the morning,
They saw Him coming toward them,
   He was walking on the water,
   But it looked like He was going to pass by them.

205. (6:49fa)
When they first saw Him, walking on the water,
They thought that it was a spirit and they screamed,
   Because all of them saw Him
   And all of them were terrified.

206. (6:50b-51)
Then immediately He spoke to them and said,
"Cheer up! It is I! Do not be afraid!" [51]
   Then, as He climbed into the boat with them,
   The wind stopped blowing.

207. (6:51bf)
And they were utterly amazed,
Because they had not understood
   What He had said to them about the loaves,
   Because their hearts had become stubborn.

Ministry in Gennesaret

208. (6:53fa)

And when they had crossed over to the other side,
They landed and tied up the boat at Gennesaret.
   But, as soon as they got out of the boat,
   Jesus was recognized.

209. (6:55)

And the people went throughout the neighborhood,
Found all those who were sick
   And brought them out on mats to wherever
   They had heard that Jesus was going to be passing.

210. (5:56)

And everywhere He went, village, town, or countryside,
They laid their sick along the way and begged him
   For permission even to touch the hem of his mantle;
   And all those who touched Him were healed.

CHAPTER 7

The Dangers of Human Traditions

211. (7:1f)
When the Pharisees gathered around Jesus,
With some scribes, who had come from Jerusalem,
    They saw that some of His disciples were eating,
    But had not washed their hands.

212. (7:3)
And the Pharisees…in fact, all the Jews,
Honor the traditions of their ancestors;[79]
    And none of them eat,
    Without washing their hands.

213. (7:4)
And when they come from the marketplace,
They do not eat until they wash their hands.
    And they strictly keep many other traditions,
    Such as, washing cups, pots, and pans of bronze.

214. (7:5)
So the Pharisees and the scribes asked Jesus,
"Why is it? That your disciples
    Do not honor the tradition of the elders,
    About eating without washing their hands?"

215. (7:6a)
And Jesus replied, "So Isaiah was correct
When he prophesied
    About you hypocrites;
    As it is written,

---

[79] Sine "Tradition" means "what has been handed down," there are both good and bad traditions.

216. (7:6bf)

This nation honors me with their lips,
But their hearts are far from me.
    Therefore, it is useless for them to worship me,
      Since their teachings are rules, that they have made.

217. (7:8f)

You forsake the commandments of God,
And keep the traditions of men.
    Yes! You find it easy to ignore God's Word,
    In order to keep your own traditions.

218. (7:10)

Moses said,
"Honor your father and your mother!"
    And "Whoever curses either father or mother
    Must surely die!"

219. (7:11)

But you say,
"Anyone can say to one's father or mother,
    'Whatever I owe to you
    Has already been given to God as an offering!'"[80]

220. (7:12)

And when that has been done,
You renounce all your obligations
    Both to your father or to your mother;
    And that shows how you oppose the Word of God.

221. (7:13)

By following your own traditions,
That are handed down to you,
    And which you gladly receive;
    You also do many other things, just like that! [14]

---

[80] Or "What you would have received from me is Corban (i.e., has been given to God)."

222. (7:14)

Then Jesus got the attention of all the people again,
And He said to them,
"Listen to me, all of you,
And understand what I am saying.

223. (7:15 f)

Nothing, from outside of you[81] can defile[82] you;
What defiles you
Is what comes out of you.
If anyone has ears to hear, let them hear."

224. (7:17-f-a)

Later, after they had left the people
And had gone into the house,
His disciples asked him about the comparison.
And this is what He said to them.

225. (7:18b-19a)

"Do you still not understand what I am saying?
No food that a person eats defiles that person,
Since it enters the stomach, and not the heart,
And, through the bowels, passes out of the body."[83]

226. (7:19b-20a)

By saying that, Jesus made all food clean;[84]
And as He continued, He said to them,
Since evil intentions come out of the human heart,
That is what defiles a person.

---

[81] That is, food.

[82] To "defile" means to make a person guilty before God.

[83] The point here is, not on the physical effect of the food, as food, but the guilt that results from eating a forbidden food. In other words, there is no forbidden food. One or another food may not be as healthy for you, but that is a different matter.

[84] The statement that "all food is clean" means that there are not two lists of food: one that you are permitted to eat and one that you are not permitted to eat; and therefore, there is no sin in eating them, but that does not mean that all food is clean, in terms of its being sanitary, or healthy.

227. (7:21b-22a)
This is clearly seen in fornication and theft,
As well as in murder and adultery,
    But also in greediness and malice,
    And in deception and self-indulgence.
228. (7:22b -23)
We could also cite the evil eye[85] and blasphemy,
And, especially, pride and foolishness;
    All these evil things come out of the heart;
    And that is what defiles a person."

In Phoenicia[86]

229. (7:24)
Then Jesus left that area and went to Tyre and Sidon,
Where He entered a house;
    But He did not want it known that He was there;
    But His presence could not be hidden.
230. (7:25)
So immediately a woman,
Whose young daughter had an evil spirit, [26]
    After hearing about Jesus,
    Came in and fell down at His feet.
231. (7:26)
She was a Greek woman,
Who had been born in Syro-Phoenicia?[87]
    And she begged Him to cast out the demon
    That was in her daughter.

---

[85] I would define "the evil eye" as "intention to do harm, looking for an opportunity to do it."

[86] Phoenicia is a province north of Galilee on the Mediterranean coast; Tyre and Sidon are its largest towns.

[87] Pronunciation: SIGH-row-feh-NEE-cian.

232. (7:27)
And Jesus said to her,
"Let the children finish eating first:
    Because it is not right to take the children's bread,
    And throw it on the floor for the puppies.

233. (7:28)
And she answered him and said,
"Yes! Your honor, you are right!
    But the puppies under the table
    Eat what the children drop on the floor."

234. (7:29)
And because she said that,
Jesus says to her,
    "You may go home;
    The demon has left your daughter."

235. (7:30)
So she went home,
And she discovered that,
    Although the child was still in bed,
    The demon had already departed. [31]

ഗ ✿ ൪

In Decapolis[88]

236. (7:31)
When Jesus left the area of Tyre,
He first went north to Sidon,
    And then took the road toward the Sea of Galilee,
    And turned east through the region of Decapolis.

---

[88] The Decapolis was the "Ten Cities" (mostly Gentile) to the east and north of the Sea of Galilee.

237. (7:32)
And there, a man, who was deaf and tongue-tied,
Was brought to Jesus,
    And they begged Jesus
    To lay His hand on him.

238. (7:33)
Then, after taking him aside from the crowd,
Jesus put His fingers into his ears,
    And when He had spit,
    He touched the man's tongue.

239. (7:34-35)
And looking up to heaven, Jesus groaned,
And said to the man, "EF-fa-THA," (i.e., "Be opened");
    And his ears were opened at once,
    And his tongue was loosened, and he spoke clearly.

240. (7:36)
Then Jesus told them,
To tell no one:
    But the more He told them,
    The more they proclaimed it, with great zeal.

241. (7:37)
Because they were amazed beyond measure,
They kept on saying, 'He has done all things well:
    He even makes those who do not hear to hear,
    And those who do not speak to speak.

CHAPTER 8

Feeding the Four Thousand

241. (8:1)

On another occasion in those days,
When a large crowd had gathered
   And they had nothing to eat,
     Jesus called his disciples, and He says to them.

242. (8:2)

'I have compassion on the people,
Because this is now the third day
   That they have been with me
   And they have not eaten.

243. (8:3)

And if I send them away,
In their present weak condition,
   They will faint on their way home;
   Because some of them have a long way to go.'

244. (8:4)

And His disciples say to Him,
"Where, in this desert, is <u>anyone</u>
   Going to find enough bread
   To feed this many people?"

245. (8:5)

Then Jesus asked them this question,
"How much bread do you have?"
   And they respond,
   "We have seven loaves of bread."

246. (8:6a)
So, after He had commanded the people
To sit down on the ground,
    Jesus takes the seven loaves,
    And gives thanks.

247. (8:6b-7a)
Then He broke the bread into pieces.
And gave the broken pieces to His disciples
    To share with the people.
    And they shared the bread with the people.

248. (8:7b)
They also had a few fish,
Which He blessed,
    And then He commanded
    That the fish be served to the people.

249. (8:8-9)
So, all of them ate,
Until they were full and satisfied;
    And there was enough food left-over
    To fill seven baskets.

250. (8:10a)
And there were about
Four thousand people who ate;
    And when they had finished,
    He sent them away.

☙ ❀ ☜
The Region near Dalma-mutha
The Pharisees Ask for a Sign
251. (8:10b)

When that was over,
Jesus got into a boat, with His disciples,
    And they went to a place
    That is near Dalma-mutha.[89]

252. (8:11)

And there the Pharisees gathered together
To argue with Jesus;
    They said that they needed a sign from heaven,
    But they were really trying to trap Him.

253. (8:12)

And after sighing deeply in His spirit, Jesus says,
"Why does this generation seek for a sign?
    I give you this… and that is my final Word,
    No sign shall be given to this generation."

☙ ❀ ☜
Beware the Leaven
Of Both the Pharisees and the Herodians
254. (8.13-15)

After dismissing the people and getting into the boat,
Jesus departed for the other side.
    But the disciples had forgotten to get bread,
    And they had only one loaf of bread in the boat.

---

[89] Pronunciation: DAL-mah-MOO-thah.

255. (8:16)
And Jesus cautioned them by saying,
"Pay attention! And guard yourselves
   Against the leaven[90] of the Pharisees,
    And the leaven of Herod."

256. (8:17)
And they began to discuss this with each other,
Thinking that it was about not having bread.
  But, Jesus, aware of this, says to them,
    "Why were you discussing 'not having bread'?"

257. (8:18)
"Do you not see or understand, even yet?
Do you still have a hard and insensitive heart?
  Although you have eyes, do you not see?
  And although you have ears, do you not hear?

258. (8:19-20a)
"Have you already forgotten?
When I broke the five loaves for the five thousand,
  How many baskets of left-over food did we have?
  And they said, "Twelve."

259. (8:20b-21)
"And the seven loaves for the four thousand,
How many baskets of fragments did you take up?"
  And they said, "Seven."
  And he says to them, "Do you still not understand?"

---

[90] Often leaven is used to symbolize sin in Scripture; here it is probably something like "the evil intent."

ೊ ✿ ഓ
On the Way to Caesarea Philippi
260. (8:22)
When Jesus arrived in Bethsaida,
The people bring a blind man to him
    And they ask Him,
    If He would, please, touch him.
261. (8:23)
After Jesus took the blind man by the hand
And led him outside the village,
    He laid His hands on him
    And spit on his eyes.
262. (8:23b-24)
Then Jesus asked him
If he could see anything.
    And the blind man looked up and says,
    "I see men, like trees, walking."[91]
263. (8:25)
Then Jesus laid His hands on his eyes again,
And told him to look up;
    And he was made whole,
    Because he could see everything clearly.
264. (8:26)
Jesus sent the man home,
With these instructions,
    "Do not go into the town;
    And do not tell anyone in the town about this."

---

[91] Some view this as a semi-failure of Jesus; rather, it is an encouragement to the man that is being healed.

Near Caesarea Philippi
Peter: "You are the Messiah!"

265. (8:27)

Then Jesus and his disciples departed and went north,
Toward the villages of Caesarea Philippi.
    On the way Jesus asked his disciples this question,
    "What are the people saying about who I am?"

266. (8:28)

And they told Him,
"Some say that You are John the Baptizer:
    Some say that You are Elijah;
    And others say that You are just a prophet.
"

267. (8:29)

Then Jesus asked them directly,
"But you! Who do *you* say that I am?"
    And Peter said to Him, "You are the Messiah."
    And Jesus ordered them not to tell that to anyone.

Part II

**The Promised Messiah
Is the Suffering Servant
8:31-End**

ಸಂ † ಜಿ

His Death and Resurrection
The First Announcement (1 of 3)

268. (8:31)

From that time on…Jesus began to teach them,
That the 'Son of Man' had to suffer many things:
   That He would be rejected by the elders,
   That is, the chief priests and the scribes.

269. (8:32a)

And that He would be killed,[92]
But also, that, on Day Three,[93]
   He would come back to life.
   And He spoke about this matter very clearly.

---

[92] This announcement (8:32) is repeated twice (9:32 and 10:34).

[93] At that time, Hebrew and Greek could count "one, two, three, etc.," but did not have the Arabic number system to represent the numbers (e.g., 1, 2, 3). The used the alphabet, with a marking (a', b' c') and they had no zero. Today was Day One, tomorrow was Day Two, etc.). So any part of the beginning and ending of a day/week/month/year was counted as a day, week, month or year. The three days here are: "Friday (crucifixion), Saturday (rest), and Sunday (resurrection). And any part of a day (which for the Jews started and ended at sunset) was counted as a day.

Peter Rebukes Jesus
270. (8:32b-33a)
At that point, Peter called Jesus aside
And began to rebuke Him.
    But Jesus looking back at his disciples,
    Rebukes Peter with these words.
271. (8:33b)
"Get behind me, Satan:
Because you are not thinking
    On the things of God;
    But on things that are carnal and earthly."

-o0o-
"What Does It Mean To be a Disciple of Jesus."
272. (8:34)
Then Jesus invited the people to come closer to Him,
Including His disciples, and He says to them,
    "If you want to be My disciple,
    Deny yourself, take up your cross, and follow me.
273. (8:35-36a)
Because if your aim is to save your life,
You will lose it
    But if you lose your life for me and the Gospel,
    You will save it.
274. (8:36-37)
Think about it! What advantage would it be to you,
If you were to gain the whole world,
    But lose your own life? And, if that were so,
    What would you pay to get your life back?

275. (8:38)
Whoever is ashamed of me and my teachings,
In this adulterous and sinful generation, of him, also,
  The Son of Man shall be ashamed, when He comes
  In the glory of His Father, with the holy angels.

CHAPTER 9

A Mighty Display of the Power of God: 9:1-29
276. (9:1)
And Jesus says to them,
"Listen! Because this is absolutely true;
   Some of you, standing here, shall not taste of death,
   Until you have the Kingdom of God revealed in power.

ꛛ ✿ ꛚ

The Transfiguration of Jesus: 9:2-8
277. (9:2)
And six days later
Jesus takes Peter, James and John
   And they go up on a high mountain,
   Apart by themselves.

278. (9:3)
And while James and John are looking at Jesus,
His whole appearance is transformed;
   All His clothing begins to glow, intensely white,
   Whiter than anyone on earth could bleach them.

279. (9:4 -5)
Then Elijah and Moses appear;
And begin to speak with Jesus;
   And Peter says to Jesus,
   "Rabbi, it is good for us to be here!

280. (9:6)
Let us make three tents:
One for You; one for Moses; and one for Elijah!"
   Peter said this, not knowing what else to say;
   Sense he was terrified, along with James and John.

281. (9:7)
Then a cloud, completely, covered them;
And a voice, out of the cloud, said,
   "This is my beloved Son!
   Love and obey Him!"

282. (9:8)
And, all of a sudden,
As they are looking,
   They became aware, that, except for Jesus,
   No one else is with them.

The Question about Elijah
9:9-13

283. (9:9)
As they were coming down from the mountain,
Jesus commands them not to tell anyone
   About what they had seen,
   Until the Son of Man is raised from the dead.[94]

284. (9:10-11)
So they did not talk about it, but they wondered
What being raised from the dead could mean.
   So they asked him, saying, "Why do the scribes say
   That Elijah has to come first?"

285. (9:12)
Jesus replied, "Elijah comes first to restore all things;
But what does Scripture say about the Son of Man?
   He must suffer many things
   And be treated with disrespect and contempt.

---

[94] This statement is a clear witness (1) that Jesus identified Himself as the "Son of Man" and (2) that Peter is the source of Mark's information.

286. (9:13)

But I say to you,
'Elijah has already come,
    And they did to him what they wanted to do,
    Just as it was written about him'."

Casting Out...an Unclean Spirit
9:14-29

287. (9:14)

And when they got back
To where the other disciples were,
    They saw a lot of people around them,
    And the scribes were probing them with questions.

288. (9:15-16)

And when they see Jesus, all the people are amazed
So they come, running, to greet him.
    And He asks them,
    "What did you want my disciples to do for you?"

289. (9:17-18a)

And a man in the crowd spoke up and said,
"Teacher, I brought you my son;
    He has a spirit that does not let him speak.
    And when it comes on him, it throws him down.

290. (9:18b)

Not only does he foam at the mouth
But he also grinds his teeth and becomes rigid.
    I asked your disciples to cast it out;
    But they were not able to do so."

291. (9:19)

Jesus responded, "What an unbelieving generation!
How long am I going to be with you?
    How long must I put up with you?
    Bring him to me."

292. (9:20)

So they bring the boy to Jesus,
And when the boy sees Jesus,
    The spirit immediately throws him to the ground,
    Where he rolls around and foams at the mouth.

293. (9:21)

Then Jesus questions his father,
"How long has this been going on?"
    And the father says,
    "It has been going on since he was a child.

294. (9:22)

"Many times it throws him into the fire,
Or into the water, in order to destroy him;
    But if you can do anything,
    Please! Have mercy on us! And help us!'

295. (9:23)

And Jesus said to the man,
Did you say: 'If you can?'….
    Remember! All things are possible
    To the one who believes.

296. (9:24)

Instantly the father of the child
Cries out and says,
    "I believe! And I beg you, 'Please!'
    Help me to trust in you completely!"

297. (9:25a)
Then Jesus, seeing that a crowd
Was rapidly forming,
    Rebukes the unclean spirit,
    Saying to him,
298. (9:25b)
"You deaf and dumb spirit,
I command you:
    Come out of him,
    And never enter him again."
299. (9:26a)
And, after the evil spirit had cried out…
And had violently shaken his body,
    It came out of him;
    And it looked like…the boy was dead.
300. (9:26b-27)
This caused many of them to say,
"He is dead!"
    But Jesus, taking him by the hand,
    Helps him; and the boy stands up.
301. (9:28)
After Jesus went into the house with His disciples
They asked him in private,
    "Why were we not able
    To cast out the evil spirit?"
302. (9:29)
And Jesus says to them,
"There is no way
    To cast out this kind,
    Except through prayer and fasting[95]."

---

[95] "Through prayer and fasting": Some Bibles have this reading, and others just have "through prayer." On "Bible Gateway" (Online) five different texts of the Greek New Testaments (NT) are available for consultation. Three have

His Death and Resurrection
The Second Announcement (2 of 3)
303. (9:30)
After that, they continued
Their journey through Galilee;
    But He did not want anyone to know about it.
    Since He was teaching His disciples about His death.
304. (9:31-32)
"The Son of Man shall be delivered into hands of men,
And they will kill Him;
    However, on Day Three He shall be raised."
    But they did not understand and were afraid to ask.

The Measure of Greatness
305. (9:33)
When they got back to Capernaum
And were in the house,
    Jesus asked His disciples,
    "What were you discussing as we returned?"

"prayer and fasting" (Stephanus, (1550), Scrivener Greek NT (1894), and Tyndale House Greek NT). Two of the five do not add "and fasting: Westcott & Hort Greek NT, 1891 and SBL (Society for Biblical Studies) Greek NT. This is generally considered as due to the discovery of two manuscripts (that did not contain the additional two words): the Vaticanus and the Sinaiticus, both produced in the fourth century. But Jesus considered kingdom life as firmly founded on prayer and fasting. In the second of the three chapters in his Sermon on the Mount in Matthew (chapter 6), Jesus follows His teaching on prayer with teaching on fasting. So what does this verse mean, if it does not include fasting? Jesus had already given them authority to cast out demons, but demons are personalities, and some put up more resistance than others.

306. (9:34)
And no one said a word,
Because on the way back
   They had argued about…
    "Who is the greatest among us?"
307. (9:35)
And when He had taken His seat
He calls the twelve and says to them,
   Anyone, who wants to be the first,
    Shall be the last of all *and* the servant of all."
308. (9:36)
Then He sends for a child,
And has it stand before them:
   And, as He hugs the child,
    He says to them,
309. (9:37)
"Whoever welcomes just one child, like this,
"In my name, welcomes me:
   And whoever welcomes me,
    Welcomes not me, but Him who sent me."

ಏ ❀ ಐ

For Us or Against Us?
310. (9:38)
John said to Jesus, "Master, we saw someone,
Who was casting out demons in Your Name,
   And we told him not to do that,
    Because he is not one of us."

311. (9:39-40)
But Jesus said, "Do not hinder him:
Because no one, who does a miracle in my name,
    Shall be able, soon after that, to speak evil of me.
    For whoever is not against us is for us.

312. (9:41)
What I am telling you is absolutely true!
Whoever gives you a cup of water to drink,
    Because you bear the name of Christ,
    Shall not lose their reward.

ಸ ❀ ಆ

Faithfulness to Jesus

313. (9:42)
It would be better to have a millstone,
Locked around your neck and to be cast into the sea,
    Than to cause one of these little ones,
    Who trust in Me, to turn back and not trust in Me.

314. (9:43-44a)
If your hand causes you to turn back, cut it off:
For it is better to enter into life with one hand,
    Than with two hands, to be thrown into hell,
    Where the fire never goes out.

315. (9:45-46
If your foot causes you to turn back, cut it off:
For it is better for you to enter into life with one foot,
    Than with two feet, to be thrown into hell,
    Where the fire never goes out.

316. (9:47-48)
And if your eye causes you to turn back, pull it out;
For it is better to enter God's kingdom with one eye,
> Than with two eyes, to be thrown into hell,
> Where the fire never goes out.

ಞ ❈ ಆ

Salt
317. (9:49-50)
Salt is good, because everything hall be salted by fire;
But if it loses its strength,[96] how can it serve as salt?
> May your life together be seasoned with salt!
> So that you may live together in peace.

---

[96] Salt is both a preservative and a seasoning, in both cases it functions to the benefit of that to which it is applied. Note the parallel to agape love.

CHAPTER 10

Teaching about Divorce

318. (10:1)

After He left there[97], He went to Judea,
To the section east of the Jordan River;
    And, as usual, large crowds gathered around Hm;
    And He began to teach them.

319. (10:2-3)

Some Pharisees came to test Him, and asked,
"Is it lawful for a man to divorce his wife?"
    Then Jesus answered them by saying,
    "What did Moses command you to do?"

320. (10:4-5)

And they said, 'Moses permits divorce for a man,
If, it is certified by a certificate of divorce. [5]
    And Jesus said to them, "He wrote this for you.
    Because your hearts are hard .[6]

321. (10:6-7-8a)

"In the beginning God made them male and female.
Therefore a man leaves his father and his mother,
    And is joined to his wife; [8]
    And the two of them become one flesh.

322. (10: 8b-9)

"Thus they are no longer two
But they are one flesh.
    Therefore, what God has joined together,
    Let no one separate."

---

[97] That is, Galilee. He generally used the road east of the Jordan River.

323. (10:10-11a)
However, once they were alone, in private,
His disciples questioned Him
    About this matter;
    And this is what Jesus taught them.

324. (10:11b-12)
"Whoever divorces his wife, and marries another,
Commits adultery against her. and
    If a wife divorces her husband and marries again,
    She commits adultery.

ഌ ❀ ಜ

Little Children Blessed

325. (10:13)
One day, when some of the people
Brought their children to Jesus,
    For Him to lay hands on them,
    His disciples rebuked them.

326. (10:14a)
But when Jesus saw it,
He was annoyed and said to them,
    "Let the children draw near and come to me!
    And do not hinder them!

327. (10:14b-15)
Because they have a right to enter God's Kingdom;
And the truth is: only those
    Who receive God's Kingdom, like a child,
    Shall be able to enter it."

328. (10:16)
So Jesus took the children
Into His arms,
    Laid His hands on them,
    And blessed them.

ೞ ✿ ಛ

The Rich Man

329. (10:17)
On day as Jesus was going out to minister,
A man came running to Him,
    Knelt down, and said to Him, "Good Teacher,
    What shall I do to inherit eternal life?"

330. (10:18)
And Jesus said to him,
"Why do you call me good?
    Because there is only One who is good
    And that is, God. [19]

331. (10:19)
"You know the commandments,
Do not commit adultery,
    Do not murder,
    Do not steal.

332. (10:20)
Do not be a false witness,
Do not deceive
    And, especially, this:
    Honor your father and your mother." [98]

---

[98] Love and honor are the glue that binds the generation together.

333. (10:21)
The man answered and said to Jesus, "Master,
I have done all these things since I was a boy."
  Then Jesus looked at him with compassion,
  And said to him,

334. (10:22)
"One thing you still lack:
Go sell what you have, and give it to the poor;
  Then you shall have treasure in heaven:
  After that, come back and follow me."

335. (10:22)
But when the man heard those words,
He was very troubled;
  And he went away sad,
  Because he was very wealthy.

ഓ ❀ ഇ

On Trusting in Riches

336. (10:23)
Then Jesus, looking around, says to His disciples,
"Oh! How hard it is for those who trust in riches,
  To let God be the King of their lives!"[99]
  And his disciples were amazed at what he said.

337. (10:24)
Then Jesus, looking round about Him,
Says to them, again,
  "Children, how hard it is,
  To let God be the King of your lives!

---

[99] Or …those who have riches to enter the Kingdom of God."

338. (10:25)
"It is easier for a camel
To go through the eye of a needle,
   Then for a rich man
    To enter in to the Kingdom of God!"
339. (10:26-27a)
Now his disciples were absolutely astonished,
And they said to Him,
   "So who can be saved?"
   And Jesus looked at them and said this.
340. (10:27b)
"With you, that is impossible,
But it is not impossible with God:
   Because with God
   All things are possible!"

ಲ ✻ ಐ
Peter's Question
341. (10:28-29a)
Then Peter spoke up and said to him,
"Look, we left everything to follow you!"
   To which Jesus responded,
   "Listen to me! This is the absolute truth!"
342. (10:29b)
"No one, who has left home,
Or brothers and sisters, or father and mother,
   Or wife, children and real estate,
   Because of Me and the Gospel,

343. (10:30a)
Shall fail to receive a hundred times as much,
Both NOW in this time: Houses, and brothers,
    And sisters, and mothers, and children,
    And real estate—BUT with persecutions,

344. (10:30b-31)
AND, in the world to come,
Eternal life. [31]
    BUT many that are first here shall be last there;
    And many that are last here shall be first there."

His Death and Resurrection
The Third Announcement (3 of 3)

345. (10:32)
As they were on their way to Jerusalem
Jesus was walking ahead of them,
    And the disciples, as they followed,
    Were troubled and afraid.

346. (10:33)
So Jesus took the twelve
And began to explain to them, again,
    What was going to happen to Him,
    And this is what He said.

347. ((10:33a))
"Remember! We are going up to Jerusalem!
And the Son of man shall be delivered
    Into the hands of the chief priests, and the scribes;
    And they shall condemn him to death.[100]

348. (10:33b-34)
"Then, they shall deliver Him to the Gentiles,
Who will mock Him, scourge Him,
    Spit on Him, and kill Him.
    But on Day Three, He will rise again.

ஐ ✿ ଔ

The Request of James and John
10:35-45

349. (10:35)
Then James and John, the sons of Zebedee,
Come to him, saying,
    "Master, we want you to do for us
    What we are going to ask You to do."

350. (10:36-37)
So Jesus said to them,
"What do you want me to do for you?"
    They said to him, "In your glory, let us to sit,
    One at your right hand and the other at your left."

351. (10:38)
Then Jesus said to them,
"You do not know what you are asking for;
    Can you drink the cup that I shall drink?
    Or be baptized the way I shall be baptized?"

---

[100] Note: They cannot execute Him, but they can condemn Him to death,

352. (10:39)

And they said to him, "We can."
So Jesus says to them,
   "Yes, indeed! You shall drink the cup that I drink
   And you shall be baptized the way I am baptized.

353. (10:40)

"But to sit at my right hand or at my left hand…
That is not mine to give;
   It will be given, only to those
   For whom it is prepared."

354. (10:41)

And when the other ten disciples heard about this,
They became very upset with James and John.
   Then Jesus, after sending for James and John,
   Says to all of them,

355. (10:42)

"You know that those who rule the nations
Act as dictators over them;
   And their, so-called, great leaders
   Misuse their authority over them.

356. (10:43-44)

But that is not a choice for you. Rather…
The one who wants to be great must be your servant;
   And the one who wants to be first among you
   Must be a slave for all the rest of you.

357. (10:45)

Because even the Son of Man
Did not come to be served,
   But to serve
   And to give his life as a ransom for all."

Day One *of* Holy Week,
(Sunday, Nisan 9)

The Healing of Blind Bartimaeus

358. (10:46)

And then they came to Jericho;
And as Jesus was leaving Jericho,
   With His disciples and many others,
     A blind man named Bartimaeus [101] sat begging.

359. (10:47)

And when he heard
That Jesus of Nazareth was passing by,
   He began yelling and said,
     "Jesus, Son of David, have mercy on me!" [4]

360. (10:48)

Many of those near him rebuked him,
And tried to make him stop yelling,
   But he yelled out all the more,
     "Son of David, have mercy on me!"

361. (10:49)

So Jesus stops and says, "Call him!"
So they call out and say to the blind man,
   "Hey, man, you can be happy!
   Get up! He's calling for you."

---

[101] Mark inserted "the son of Timaeus' as a translation of the name.

362. (10:50-51)

So he jumped up, dropped his mantle,
And went, as fast as he could, toward Jesus.
    Then Jesus said to him,
        "What do you want me to do for you?"

363. (10:52a)

And the blind man says to him,
"Master, I want to see again." 52
    And Jesus says to him,
        Go! Your faith has made you well!"

364. (10:52b)

And at that very moment
He received his sight,
    And he followed Jesus on the way,
    As He was going up to Jerusalem.[102]

---

[102] Jericho is 780 ft. below sea level and Jerusalem is 2,474 ft above sea level, a difference of 3,254 feet. And the distance is 17 miles.

CHAPTER 11

"Up to Jerusalem"
365. (11:1a)

When they got to Beth-phage,
A village near Jerusalem,
   Jesus sent two of His disciples
   On an errand to Bethany.

366. (11:1b.-2a)

Bethany was the next village
on the Mount of Olives.
   And He said to them,
   "Go ahead to the next village.

367. (11:2b-3

And when you get there,
You will find a Donkey,
   That has never been ridden,
   It is tied to a post.

368. (11:3)

"Untie the donkey and bring it to me!
And if anyone objects to what you are doing
   Tell them, 'The Lord has need of it,
   And He will return it soon.'"

369. (11:4)

So they went to Bethany,
And found the donkey, tied, near a door,
   In the open street;
   So they untied it.

370. (11:5)
And someone, standing nearby,
Saw it and said to them,
> "Hey! What are you doing…
> Untying the donkey?"

371. (11:6-7)
But when they replied
As Jesus had commanded them to reply:
> They were given permission;
> And they brought the donkey to Jesus.

-o0o-
The Royal Entry
372. (11:8a)
Then they laid their mantles on it,
And Jesus mounted the donkey.
> Many others spread out their mantles on the road:
> And still others spread branches, cut in the fields.

373. (11:8b-9)
Both those ahead and those behind
Chanted together, "Hosanna!!
> Blessed is He who comes
> In the name of the Lord!

374. (11:9b-10)
Blessed be the coming kingdom
Of our Father David!
> Hosanna in the highest!"
> And that is how He entered Jerusalem!

375. (11:11)
And Jesus went straight to the temple,
Where He looked around and sized up the situation.
> But since it was already late,
> He went back to Bethany with the Twelve.

Day Two *of* Holy Week, (Monday, Nisan 10)

The Cursing of the Fig Tree
76. (11:12)
The next day when they left Bethany,
Jesus was hungry;
    And He saw a fig-tree with green leaves on it.
    But it was off at a distance.
377. (11:13)
So He went over to see,
If, perhaps, He might find some fruit.
    But when he got to it,
    He found nothing but leaves.
378. (11:14)
That was because it was not the season for figs.
But He still said to the fig tree,
    "Let no one eat of your fruit again, forever!"
    And his disciples heard it.

❧ ✿ ☙
Cleansing the Temple

379. (11:15-16a)

When they arrived in Jerusalem,
Jesus went straight to the temple and went in;
   And He drove out those who were selling,
   As well as those who were buying.

380. (11:16b)

He overturned the tables of the moneychangers
And the seats of those who were selling doves.
   And He did not allow anyone
   To carry anything through the temple.[103]

381. (11:17a)

And while He was teaching,
He said to them, "Is it not written?"
   'My house shall be called
   The House of Prayer for All Nations!"

382. (11:17b)

But you have turned it
Into a "clubhouse"
   For those who steal
   And those who are armed bandits."

❧ ✿ ☙
Reaction to His Activity

383. (11:18a)

When the chief priests and the scribes
Heard about this,
   . . .
   They feared Him,
   And looked for a way to destroy Him.

---

[103] i.e., probably, "temple mount."

384. (11:18b-19)
But the people were enchanted
With His teaching…
    And each day, after sunset,
    He and His disciples would leave the city.

Day Three *of* Holy Week, (Tuesday, Nisan 11)

The Lesson
From the Withered Fig Tree

385. (11:20)

The next morning,
As they were coming into the city,
    They saw that the fig tree had withered,
    Even down to its roots.

386. (11:21)

This amazed Peter,
And he said to Jesus,
    "Look, Master,
    The fig tree you cursed has withered."

387. (11:22-23a)

Jesus responded,
"Have faith in God.
    Because, what I am telling you
    Is absolutely true:

388. (11:23b)

Whoever says to this mountain, without wavering in the heart,
'Be removed and be cast into the sea!'
    And truly believes that what he says is coming to pass,
    It shall be done.

388. (11:24)

"Therefore, I say to you,   11.24
'Whatever you ask for in prayer,
   Believe that you have received it,
   And it shall be yours.'

℅ ❀ ☙
Forgiveness Opens the Heart
389. (11:25)

"And as you stand praying,   11.25
If you have anything against anybody, forgive it,
   So that your Father in heaven
   May also forgive you your failures.[104]

℅ ❀ ☙
The Authority of Jesus Questioned
390. (11:27)

So they arrive again in Jerusalem:
And as Jesus was entering the temple,
   The chief priests and the scribes,
   That is, the elders, approach Him.

---

[104] Some versions, including the King James, add verse 26, which is the negative of the above, but it adds nothing to the meaning, "But if you do not forgive, neither will your Father, who is in heaven, forgive your trespasses." This is to be understood a follows: the heart has a door that must be opened from the inside. If it is not open to give forgiveness, then it is not open to receive forgiveness. An open door gives and receives forgiveness.

391. (11:28-29)
And they say to him, "By what authority
Do you do these things?
    And who gave you the authority
    To do these things?"

392. (11:30)
Jesus replied, "I also have a question for you,
And, first, you must answer me;
    Then I will tell you
    By what authority I do these things.

393. (11:31a)
"The baptism of John…
Was it from heaven?[105]
    Or was it from man?
    Answer me."

394. (11:31b)
And they argued among themselves, saying,
"If we say, from heaven,
    Then He will say,
    Why did you not believe him?

395. (11:32)
'But can we say, from man…?"
They did this because they were afraid of the people,
    Because everybody believed
    That John was a true prophet.

396. (11:33)
So, they say to Jesus, "We do not know."
Then Jesus says to them,
    "Neither will I tell you,
    By what authority I do these things."

---

[105] To avoid desecration of the Name of God, the Jews used substitutes to refer to God, like the work, "Heaven" or "Hashem" = the name).

CHAPTER 12

Still Teaching in the Temple

-o0o-
The Parable of the Vineyard: 12:1-12

397. (12:1a)
Then Jesus began to teach them,
By telling them a story.
  "A man planted a vineyard
  And he built a wall around it.
398. (12:1b)
"After that, he built a winepress in the rock,
As well as a watchtower,
  Then he hired some caretakers,
  And He, himself, went to live in another place.
399. (12:2)
"But when the time of the harvest came,
He sent a servant to his employees,
  So that he might receive
  Some of the fruit of the vineyard.
400. (12:3-4)
"But they grabbed him, and they beat him;
And they sent him away with nothing.
  Then the owner sent a different servant,
  Who was beaten on the head and mistreated.
401. (12:5)
"Then once again he sent another;
And that one they killed;
  And many others,
  Who were either beaten or killed.
402. (12:6)

"But he still had one more servant,
His Beloved Son;
    So last of all he sent him to them, saying,
    "They will respect my Son."
                      403. (12:7a)

"But those employees
Said to each other,
    "This is the heir!
    Come, let us kill him!
                      404. (12:7b-8)

"Then the inheritance will be ours."
So they grabbed him
    And they killed him
    And they cast him out of the vineyard.
                      405. (12:9)

"So, what shall the owner do about his vineyard?
He will come;
    And He will destroy them;
    And He will give the vineyard to others.
                      406. (12:10-11)

"Have you not read this?
The rejected stone became the corner stone:
    This is from the Lord,
    And it is marvelous in our eyes?"
                      407. (12:12)

They wanted to arrest him, because they knew
That he had spoken that parable against them;
    But they feared the people;
    So they left him and went their way

Paying Taxes to Caesar:

408. (12:13-14a)

Then a committee of Pharisees and Herodians
Was sent to Jesus, looking for a basis to accuse Him
    And when they arrived, they say to Him,
    "Teacher, we know that you are sincere and frank.

409. (12:14b)

"You are not swayed by the opinion of others,
Because you do not speak to please men,
    But rather, you teach the way of God
    As it really is!

410. (12:14c-15a)

"So, is it lawful for us to honor Caesar
By paying the annual head tax or no?
    Should we pay it?
    Or should we not pay it?"[106]

411. (12:15b)

Since Jesus saw that they were not sincere,
He says to them, "Why are you putting *me* on the spot?
    Show me a piece of Roman money,[107]
    So that I may see it."

412. (12:15c-16)

So they showed Him a Roman coin;
And He says to them,
    "Whose image and inscription is this?"
    They respond, "That is the image of Caesar."

---

[106] This question to Jesus also reflects an attitude that will lead to the revolt against Rome in A.D. 66 and to the destruction of the temple in A.D. 70.

[107] The Word in the Greek text is denarius, which was the standard Roman silver coin both before and after the New Testament period. The name of the coin is derived from the Latin Word "deni" (concerning ten). In the time of Jesus the value was something like a day's wages.

413. (12:17a)
So Jesus said to them,
"What bears the image of Caesar
   Belongs to Caesar,
     So give to Caesar what belongs to Caesar.
414. (12:17b)
"But what bears the image of God
Belongs to God,
   So give to God what belongs to God."
   And they were utterly amazed at Jesus.

☙ ❀ ❧

The Question about the Resurrection
415. (12:18)
Then some Sadducees came to Jesus;
They are the ones who say,
   "There is no resurrection from the dead!"
   And they put this question to Him.
416. (12:19)
"Master, Moses wrote for us, *If a man's brother dies*
And leave his wife a widow, but leaves no children,
   Then his brother should take his wife
   And raise up a family for his brother.
417. (12:20)
Once there were seven brothers; the first one married
But he died and left no children.
   Then the second brother took as wife
   But he also died and left no children.

418. (12:21-22)
And so it was with the third:
And all the seven brothers married her;
    But all of them died and left no children;
    Finally, the woman also died.

419.(12:23)
So, in the resurrection,
When all of them are raised from the dead,
    Since all seven of them were married to her,
    Whose wife shall she be?

420. (12:24)
And Jesus answered them by saying,
Is this not the reason that you are deceived,
    Because you do not know the Scriptures
    Nor the power of God?

421. (12:25)
Because when people are raised from the dead,
They neither marry.
    Nor are given into marriage;
    But they are like the angels in heaven.

422. (12:25a)
But as to whether or not,
There is a resurrection from the dead...
    In the Book of Moses, in the passage about the bush,
    Did you never read what God said to Moses?

423.
'I am the God of Abraham,
The God of Isaac, and the God of Jacob!'
    He is not the God of the dead, but of the living;
    So, you are very much deceived.

The Great Commandment
12:28-34

424. (12:28)
Then one of the scribes,
After he had heard all the questions
    And saw that Jesus had answered them well,
    Asked him this question.

425. (12:28b-29a)
"Of all the commandments,
Which one is the most important of all?"
    And Jesus gave him this answer,
    "The most important commandment of all is this.

426. (12:29b)
"Hear, O Israel:
The LORD is our God!
    And the LORD is the only
    One, True, Living God.

427. (12:30)
And you shall love the Lord your God
With all your entire heart, i.e., your entire being,
    With all your mind,
    And with all your strength.

428. (12:331)
And the second one is this:
You shall love your neighbor as yourself.
    There is no other commandment
    More importance than these two.

429. (12:32)

And the scribe replied, "That is well said, Master!
You have spoken the truth:
   Because there is only one God;
   And there is no other god, apart from Him.

430. (12:33a)

And we are to love Him with all our heart,
With all our understanding,
   With all our soul and
   With all our strength.

431. (12:33b)

"And we are to love our neighbor,
As we love ourselves.
   That is more important than the whole system
   Of burnt offerings and sacrifices."

432. (12:34)

And when Jesus saw that he understood
And answered correctly, He said to him,
   "You are not far from God's Kingdom."
     And after that, no one dared to ask Him anything.

ಸಾ 📖 ಜ
The Question that Jesus Asked

433. (12:35-36)

So, as Jesus continued to teach in the temple
He spoke up and said, "How can the scribes say,
   That the Messiah is David's Son?
   Because David himself, by the Holy Spirit, said:

434. (12:37)
"The LORD said to my Lord,
'Sit here at my right hand,
    Until I subdue your enemies
    And put them under your feet.'

435. (12:37)
Since David himself calls him LORD;
How can he also be his son?"
    And the common people
    Gladly listened to Him.

ೞ ❀ ಚ

Denouncing the Scribes

436. (12:38-39)
In His teachings, Jesus said, "Beware of the scribes!
They love to wear long robes,
    To be greeted in the marketplaces,
    And to be seen in the meetings at the synagogue.

437. (12:40)
"And, at the same time, that they are robbing widows
They are praying long prayers;
    And that is how they keep on adding to
    Their future punishment.

ೞ ❀ ಚ

The Widow's Mite

438. (12:41a)
Then Jesus sat down,
Where He could see into the treasury,
    And He saw the people
    As they dropped their money into the treasury.

439. (12:41b-42)
Many of them who were rich gave a lot.
But then a certain poor widow came in;
    And she gave two small copper coins
    That were worth almost nothing.

440. (12:43)
Then Jesus got the attention of His disciples
And said to them, "I tell you the truth!
    This poor widow gave more than all the others
    Who gave money for the treasury.

441. (12:44)
"Because all the others
Gave out of their abundance,
    But she, out of her poverty,
    Gave all that she had to live on."

CHAPTER 13

The Destruction of the Temple Foretold
442. (13:1)
As Jesus was leaving the temple,
One of his disciples says to him,
"Look, Master! What magnificent stones!
Wow! What awesome buildings!"
443. (13/2)
And Jesus said to him,
"Do you see those great buildings?
Not one stone shall be left where it is;
Every last one of them shall be torn down."

℘ ❀ ℘

The Beginning of Woes
444. (13:3a)
While sitting on the Mount of Olives,
Looking back and viewing the temple,
Peter, James, John and Andrew
Said to Him in private,
445. (13:3b-4)
"Tell us;
When is this going to happen?
And what is the sign of the time
When all these things are about to happen?"
446. (13.5-6)
Then Jesus began and said to them,
"Be very careful! Or someone will deceive you.
Many shall come in my name, saying,
'I am he!' and they will deceive many.

☙ ✣ ❧
447. (13:7)
So when you hear of wars,
And everybody is talking about war,
    Do not be alarmed, because that has to be;
    But…that is not yet the end.

448. (13:8a)
Because nation shall rise up against nation,
And kingdom against kingdom;
    And there shall be earthquakes in many places,
    As well as famines;

449. (13:8b-9a)
These things are only the beginning of the birth pains.
So, always be alert, for your own safety;
    Because they are going to arrest you,
    Put you on trial and beat you in the synagogues.

450. (13:9b-10)
You shall also be brought before rulers,
Because of me, as a witness to them.
    But, first of all, this gospel must be preached
    To all the nations.

☙ ✣ ❧
451. (13:11)
And when they arrest you and bring you to trial,
Do not worry about what you are going to say.
    But speak what is given to you at that moment;
    Because it is not you who speak, but the Holy Spirit.

452. (13:12)
A brother shall hand over his brother to be killed,
And a father his child;
    Children shall rebel against their parents
    And be the cause of their death.

453. (13:13)
And you shall be hated by everybody,
Because you bear my name:
    But the one, who holds out to the end,
    Is the one, who hall be saved.

ಸಾ ✿ ಲ

The Great Tribulation

454. (13:14)
But when you see "The Shameless, False Worship,"
Set up where it ought not to be ((let the reader understand)
    That is the time for those in Judea
    To flee immediately to the mountains.

455. (13:15-16)
If one happens to be on the roof,
Do not enter the house to take anything,
    And, if one is at work in the field
    Do not go back to the house, even to get one's mantle

.456. (13:17-18)
In those days, woe to the women who are pregnant!
And woe to those who have a nursing child!
    Pray that your departure
    May not occur during the time of winter.

457. (13:19)
Because then… there shall be suffering and sorrow,
Like nothing that has ever been seen before,
    From the beginning of God's creation up to now,
    And never shall be again.

458. (13:20)
And unless the Lord shortens those days,
No living creature shall be saved:
    But for the sake of the elect, whom he has chosen,
    He will shorten those days.

ഉ ❀ ഇ

459. (13:21)
At that time, if anyone says to you,
"Look! The Messiah is here!"
    Or "Look! He is there!"
    Do not believe that person.

460. (13:22-23)
Because false Messiahs and false prophets shall arise
And they shall perform signs and wonders
    To deceive, even the elect, if possible…
    But note! I have already told you all these things.

ഉ ❀ ഇ

The Coming of the Son of Man

461 (13:24)
But in those days
The days after that tribulation,
    The sun shall be darkened,
    And the moon shall not give its light.

462. (13:24-25)
The stars of heaven shall fall,
And its powers shall be shaken.
    Then the Son of man will be seen,
    Coming in the clouds with great power and glory.

463. (13:27)
Then, He shall send His angels and gather His elect,
From the north, the south, the east and the west,
> From the most remote parts of the earth
> To the most remote parts of heaven.[108]

ಸಿ ❀ ಲ

The Lesson of the Fig Tree
464. (13:28)
Learn a lesson from the fig tree.
As soon as its branches become tender
> And its leaves begin to sprout,
> You know that summer is near.

465 (13:29-30a)
So also, when you see these things happen,
Be assured that He is near,
> Even at the door.
> What I am telling you is absolutely true!

466. (13:30b-31)
This generation may or may not pass[109] away,
As it waits for all these things to happen.
> Even Heaven and earth shall pass away;
> But my Words shall not pass away.

---

[108] That is, "the living" (on earth) and "the dead" (in heaven).

[109] This verb in Greek is in the aorist tense (this shows the action all at once, like "bought" vs "was buying"; and it is also in the subjunctive mood (not indicative,) and indicated contingency, as in a wish, like, "I hope that so and so happens." The word "happen," in the next line, is also aorist and subjunctive.

The Day and the Hour is Unknown

467. (13:32b-33)

No one, but the Father, knows the day and the hour,
Not the angels in heaven, nor even the Son;
   So be watchful...and stay on the alert!
   Because you do not know what moment it may be.

468. (13:34)

It is like a man, going for a long journey.
Before he goes away, he leaves his servants in charge.
   Each one is given an assignment.
   And he orders the gatekeeper to keep watch.

469. (13:35)

Therefore watch, because you do not know
When the master of the house may arrive,
   Whether in the evening, or at midnight,
   Or at cockcrowing, or in the morning.[110]

470. (13:36)

May He not find you sleeping,
When He arrives unannounced.
   And what I say to you
   I say to all, "Keep your eyes open!"

---

[110] Matthew Britt, The Hymns of the Breviary and Missal (New York: Benziger Brothers, 1924), p. 32: "Roman Divisions of the Night:
   The First Watch (evening) was from 6:00 to 9:00 p.m.
   The Second Watch (midnight) was from 9:00 p.m. to 12:00 a.m.
   The Third Watch (cockcrowing) was from 12:00 to 3:00 a.m.
   The Fourth Watch (morning) was from 3:00 to 6:00 a.m....(and)...In a single verse, Mark refers to the four watches. "You know not when the lord of the house cometh; at even, or at midnight, or at the cockcrowing, or in the morning."

CHAPTER 14

Day Four of Holy Week, (Wednesday, Nisan 12)[111]

The Plot to Kill Jesus

471. (14:1)
Two days before Passover and Unleavened Bread,
The high priests and the scribes
   Were already looking for a quiet way
   To arrest Jesus and to put Him to death.

472. (14:2)
But they said,
"We must not do it during the festival,
   Because it might cause a riot
   Among the people."

The Anointing at Bethany

473. (14:3a)
While Jesus was still in Bethany,
Dining in the house of Simon the leper,
   A woman came in with a very expensive
   Alabaster jar of pure spikenard.

---

[111] Jesus did not go into Jerusalem on Wednesday.

474. (14:3b-4)
And after breaking the seal and opening the jar,
She poured what was in it, on His head.
    And some of those present were indignant and thought,
    "Why was that perfume wasted?"

475. (14:5)
That could have been sold
For more than a year's wages
    And given to the poor."
    And they were angry at the woman.

476. (14:6)
But Jesus said, "Leave her alone!
Why bother her?
    Because this is a good deed,
    That she has done for me."

477. (14:7)
You will always have the poor with you,
And whenever you want to help them,
    You can help them:
    But you will not always have me with you.

478. (14:8-9a)
She has done what she could;
She has anointed my body,
    Ahead of time, for my burial.
    And you can be sure of this…

479. (14:9b)
Wherever the gospel is preached…
Anywhere in the whole world…
    What she has done here today
    Shall be told, as a memorial to her.

Judas Agrees to Betray Jesus

480. (14:10)

Then Judas Iscariot,
Who was one of the twelve,
    Went to the chief priests,
    And agreed to lead them to Jesus.

481. (14:11)

The priests were glad to hear his offer;
And they promised to give him money;
    So he began to look for the best way
    To do that.[112]

Day Five *of* Holy Week
(Thursday, Nisan 13)

Preparing the Room in Jerusalem

482. (14:12a

It was the day before
The Feast of Unleavened Bread,[113]
    That is, it was the day before
    The Passover Lambs were to be slain.

---

[112] Planning, related to the betrayal of Jesus, was done in Jerusalem that day, but Jesus was in Bethany, attending a banquet and being anointed.

[113] This presupposes the Feast of Unleavened Bread (seven days) also included the Day of Passover, the day that the lamb was sacrificed in the afternoon; and there were two meals at Passover: (1) the night before to find and throw out the leaven and (2) the night following, when the lamb was eaten, generally known as the Passover Meal. See my "Was the Last Supper a Passover Seder?" in Passover, Pentecost and Parousia, ed. by Steven Jack Land, Rickie D. Moore and John Christopher Thomas (Blandford Forum (UK): Deo Publishing, 2910), pp. 66-89.

483. (14:12b)

His disciples say to Him.
"When we go into town,
Where do you want us to prepare
 For you to eat the Passover?"[114]

484. (14:13)

So he sends two of his disciples to take care of that.
And these are the instructions that He gave them.
 As you enter the city, you will meet a man,
 With a water-jar full of water.[115] Follow him!

485. (14:14)

And say to the head of the house where he enters,
'The Master says, "Where is the guest room,
 For me and my disciples
 To celebrate the Passover?[116]

486. (14:15)

He will show you a large upper room,
It is already furnished and in order.
 That is the place
 Where you will prepare for us.

---

[114] The Jewish day was from sunset to sunset; so Passover had two evenings, the first evening was to clear the house of leaven (the symbol of evil or sin) and the second evening was to eat the Passover meal, which included the Passover lamb. The Last Supper was on the first evening and the emphasis was on the leaven, in this case, (1) the betrayal of Judas,(2) the abandonment of all the disciples, and (3) the denial of Peter.

[115] The young man with the water-jar was probably Mark's way of referring to himself, because we know that the last supper was held in the house of Mary, the mother of Mark. The family was one of many families that had moved back to Jerusalem, and we know that parts of this family had lived in Cyprus. According to Coptic tradition the family had moved back to Jerusalem from North Africa.

[116] Since the Jewish day began and ended at sunset (dark), each day had two evenings (the first evening of Passover was focused on the removal of the leaven and the second evening to the eating of the Passover Meal); and the first evening was a preparation for the second evening.

487. (14:16)
So His disciples left and went into the city.
And there they found everything
   Just as Jesus had told them;
   So they prepared the room for the Passover.[117]

Day Six *of* Holy Week
(Friday, Nisan 14)

The First Evening of Nisan 14[118]

The Last Supper
With Focus on the "Leaven"

488. (14:17-18)
After sunset Jesus arrived, with the twelve.
And after they were seated for the meal, and eating,
   He said to them: "Listen! This is very important!
   One of you, now eating with me, will betray me."

---

[117] The disciples did not realize that the meal that night, the night before the slaughter of the lambs, would be their last meal with Jesus, that He would be crucified at nine o'clock the nest morning and would die at three o'clock as the lambs were being slaughtered.

[118] Friday began at sunset on Thursday.

489. (14:19)
When He said that, they became very sad,
And began to say to Him,
    One after the other,
    'You are not referring to me, are you?'

490. (14:20-21a)
Then he said to them, "It is one of the twelve,
One that is now dipping in the dish with me.
    Yes, indeed, the Son of Man must be betrayed,
    Just as it is written about Him.

491. (14:21b)
"But woe to that man
By whom the Son of Man is betrayed!
    It would have been better for him,
    Never to have been born."

492. (14:22)
And while they were eating,
Jesus took bread and blessed it,
    And then He broke it, and gave it to them, saying,
    "Take and eat; this is my body!"

493. (14:23-24)
Then, after taking the cup and giving thanks;
He gave it to them, and they all drank from it,
    And He said, "This is my blood of the covenant,
    Poured out for the entire world.[119]

---

[119] Greek and KJ: "all." But see BAG (p. 694) on polloi (many) without the article and Mk 10:4, "For even the Son of man came not to be ministered unto, but to minister, and to give his life a ransom for many (and parallel in Mt 20:28). Both use "many" but Paul uses (1 Tim 2:5f) "a ransom for all." In other context, compare Mark 3:10 "For he had healed many" and Mt 12:15 "and he healed them all." See Zerwick and Grosvenor, (p. 156): polloi Semitic use, not opposite "all" but denotes "all who are many."

494. (14:25)
"Listen! This is very important!
I shall not drink of the fruit of the vine,
>   Not even one more time, until that day,
>   When I drink it new[120] n the Kingdom of God."

The Scattering of the Sheep

495. (14:26-27a)
And after they had sung a psalm,[121]
They went out to the Mount of Olives.
>   And there Jesus says to them,
>   "This night, all of you shall turn away from me.

496. (14:27-28)
"Because it is written, *I will strike the shepherd,*
And the sheep shall be scattered.
>   But after I am raised from the dead,
>   I shall go before you into Galilee."

497. (14:29-30)
And Peter says, "The rest may deny you, but not me!"[122]
But Jesus says, "Listen! This day, even thus very night,
>   Before the rooster crows the second time,
>   You are going to deny me three times."

---

[120] Or "again."

[121] What they sang that night was probably Psalms 113-118, which was sung on most of the festivals of Israel. This group of psalms is called the "Hallel" Psalms. ("Hallel" is part of the Hebrew Word, "Hallelujah', and it means "praise," "lu" means "you (plural) and "iah"(the first syllable of "Yahweh, i.e., God). These psalms, characterized by the spirit of joy and thanksgiving, were, and are, still sung at Passover and several other festivals.

[122] Or "That does not include me."

498. (14:31)
And Peter protested with much insistence, saying,
"Even if I have to die with you,
   I will certainly not deny you!"
   And all the others said the same thing.

ஸ ❦ ஊ
The Prayer in Gethsemane
499. (14:32)
Then they come to a place,
That is called, "Gethsemane"
   And Jesus says to His disciples,
   "Sit here, while I go pray."
500. (14:33)
Then Jesus takes Peter, James and John along with Him
And begins to be in deep agony and distressed.   14.34
   So He says to them, "I am so overwhelmed
   With grief and sorrow, that it almost crushes me."
501. (14:35-36a)
"Stay here, and be on the look-out."
And after going a little further, He fell on the ground;
   And He prayed that, if it were possible,
   He might be spared this time of suffering.
502. (14:36b-37a)
And this is what He said, "Abba, Father,
For whom all things are possible,
   Remove this cup from me:
   But still, Your will, not mine, be done."
503. (14:37b)
Then He returns
And finds His disciples asleep
   And He says to Peter,
   "Simon, are you asleep?

504. (14:38)
You have to watch and pray,
In order not to be overcome by temptation.
    The spirit, indeed, is willing,
    But the flesh is weak.[123]

505. (14:39-40)
Then He went and prayed again the same words.
And again He came and found them sleeping,
    Because they could not keep their eyes open,
    And they did not know what to say to Him.

506. (14:41)
Finally Jesus came a third time and says to them,
"Sleep on and take your rest! The time to pray is over!
    The time has come for the Son of Man
    To be delivered…into the hands of sinners.

The Betrayal

507. (14:42-43a)
"Get up! The time has come for us to go!
Look! The one who is betraying me is nearly here."
    And at that very moment, as he was still speaking,
    Judas, one of the twelve, came up.

508. (14:43b)
There was a large crowd with him;
And they were armed with swords and clubs:
    They had been sent by the chief priests,
    The scribes and the elders.[124]

---

[123] This is another way of saying that it is easier to make a promise than it is to keep it; and, at the same time, it is a reminder that we are limited creatures.

[124] The priests representing the Temple, the scribes, the synagogue, and the elders of the Sanhedrin (allowed by Rome).

509 (14:44)

The one who was betraying Him
Had given them a signal, saying,
    "The one I kiss is the one you want;
    Arrest Him and lead Him away safely."

510. (14:45-46)

Thus, as soon as Judas arrived,
He went straight to Jesus,
And said, "Rabbi!" as he kissed Him;
    So they took Jesus into custody.

511. (14:47)

Then one of those standing by
Drew his sword,
    Struck the servant of the high priest,
    And cut off his ear.

512. (14:48)

And Jesus, in response, said to them,
"Have you come out to arrest me,
    With swords and clubs,
    As though I were a bandit?"

513. (14:49-50)

"Day after day I was with you, teaching in the temple.
But you did not arrest me; however, it was necessary
    Because the Scriptures must be fulfilled."
    And they all abandoned Him and ran away.

ಸಾ ⚜ ಆ
The Young Man Who Fled[125]
514. (14:51-52)

A certain young man had followed Jesus to the garden,
Wearing only a mantle, over his underwear;[126] and
> When the young men who came grabbed his mantle,
> He escaped and ran away in his underwear.[127]

ಸಾ ⚜ ಆ
Jesus before the Council
515 (14:53)

Then they led Jesus away
To the palace of the high priest,
> Where all the chief priests,
> Along with the elders, and scribes were assembled.

---

[125] It is generally thought that this was Mark, because (1) the "upper Room" was in the house of his mother, Mary, and (2) this is the only gospel to contain the story.

[126] A man's clothing in the time of Jesus consisted of two parts: (1) the underwear and (2) the clothing. We find a definition of underwear in Exodus 28.42 ("Make them linen breeches to cover their nakedness from the waist to the thighs" JMB), where instructions are given for making the garments for the priest, It could have looked like anything from short shorts to Bermuda shorts. And the clothing was (1) a robe (usually tubular, floor-length, with long sleeves) and (2) a fairly large blanket to cover one while sleeping at night, or to protect one from the cold during the day.

[127] The Greek text has "naked"; but it is generally understood as parallel to the English usage, "naked" (without the outer garments) and not "stark naked" (with absolutely nothing). However, the Greek gymnastics were done naked. The reason Mark followed Jesus was that he had probably already "gone to bed" and was asleep when Jesus and His apostles were leaving. So for whatever reason decided to follow them and did not take the time to put on his robe in order not to lose their trail.

516. (14:54)
And Peter followed Him, although at a distance,
Right into the courtyard of the high priest:
    Where, he sat down with the hired servants,
    And warmed himself by the fire.
517. (14:55)
Now the chief priests, with the entire Sanhedrin,[128]
Were looking for sufficient evidence
    In order to ask for the death penalty for Jesus;
    But they found nothing.[129]
518. (14:56-57)
Many people bore false witness against Him,
But they did not agree;
    Then certain ones stood up…and
    This is the false witness they brought against Him.
519. (14:58)
"We heard Him say, 'I will destroy this temple
That was made with hands,
    And on the third day I will build another
    That is not made with hands.'"
520. (14:59-60)
But even so, their testimonies did not agree…so
The high priest stood up and questioned Jesus, directly,
    "Are you not going to give any answer at all?
    What about all these charges against you?"

---

[128] The Sanhedrin (pronounced: san-HEE-dren) was the highest religious court in Israel. But remember the Romans are in control and they handled all civil matters and the death sentence.

[129] Since the Jewish authorities could not execute Jesus, they were looking for an acceptable legal basis so that Pilate would execute Him.

521. (14:61)
But Jesus was still silent and gave them no answer.
So the high priest asked him a second question,
    Saying to Him, "Are you the Messiah,
    The Son of the Blessed One?"

522. (14:62)
And Jesus said, "I am!
And you shall see the Son of Man
    Seated at the Right Hand of the Almighty[130],
    And coming in the clouds of Heaven."[131]

523. (14:63-64)
Then the high priest said, as he tore his mantle,
"Why do we need any more witnesses?
    You have heard His blasphemy.
    What do you think?"

524. (14:65)
Then they all condemned Him, as deserving to die,
And some of them began to spit on Him;
    They cover His face, slap Him and say, 'Prophesy!'
    And even the guards strike Him, as they take Him.

☙ ✤ ❧

Peter's Denial of Jesus

525. (14:67-a
Then Peter goes downstairs
And while in the courtyard,
    One of the maids of the high priest
    Comes out into the courtyard.

---

[130] The Greek text has "Power"; Daniel 7.13 has "Ancient of Days." Both of thee and my translation ("Almighty") are ways of referring to God and not ways of addressing God (cf Jewish avoidance of the Holy Name).

[131] Here Jesus is citing Daniel 7.13.

526. (14:7b)

She sees Peter, warming himself by the fire,
And she stares at him for a moment;
    And then she says,
        "You, also, follow Jesus of Nazareth."

527. (14:68)

But he denied it, saying,
"I don't know what you're talking about."
    Then he went out near the Entry Gate;
    And the rooster crowed.

528. (14:69-70a)

Then another maid sees Peter,
And she begins to say to those standing nearby,
    "That guy is one of them!"
    But Peter denies it again

529. (14:70b)

A little later, someone standing there
Says to Peter, "You have to be one of them,
    Because you are from Galilee,
    Your speech betrays you."[132]

530. (14:71-72a)

But he began to curse and to swear, saying,
"I do not know this man of whom you speak."
    Then the rooster crowed a second time.
    And Peter remembered what Jesus had said to him,

531. (14:72b)

"Before the rooster crows a second time,
You will have denied me three times."
    And as he thought about it,
    He began to weep.

---

[132] They knew that by the way he talked.

CHAPTER 15

Jesus before Pilate

532. (15:1)
Next morning, early, the chief priests had a meeting
With the elders, scribes and the entire Sanhedrin.[133]
   Then they bound Jesus with chains
   And they led Him away.

533. (15:2)
When they turned Him over to Pilate,[134]
Pilate asked Him, "Are you the King of the Jews?"
   And the answer of Jesus was,
   "[Is that what] you say?"[135]

534. (15:3-4a)
Then, as the chief priests continued
To accuse him of many things,
   Pilate said to Him again,
   "Do you have no answer at anything?"

535: (15:4b-5)
"Look at all the charges
That they are making against you."
   But, to the amazement of Pilate,
   Jesus did not say a word.

---

[133] There were seventy-one (71) members in the Sanhedrin.

[134] Since Mark was in the final stages of putting together what turned out to be our first gospel, during of the First Jewish Revolt [AD 66-70], he)
...was challenged by two problems that affected the emerging movement of the followers of Jesus: (1) Jesus had died by crucifixion, a punishment that was reserved for treason against Rome, and (2) the followers of Jesus had to survive in the Roman Empire (from World History Encyclopedia: Pontius Pilate---online).

[135] The Greek text has only two words, "you say" (and the verb is present tense. I take this answer as "Yes!" [But not as the people want you to understand it, i.e. as a present threat to you].

ꙅ ❀ ꙅ
Jesus Sentenced to Die

536. (15:6-7)
At each Passover feast Pilate had make it a custom
To release one prisoner, chosen by the people;
    At that time there was a prisoner, called Barabbas.[136]
    He was a murderer, involved in a recent uprising.

537. (15:8-9)
After a crowd had formed, they began to cry out
That Pilate would do for them what he usually did.
    So Pilate answered them by saying,
    "Do you want me to release the King of the Jews?"

538. (15:10-11)
Pilate said that because he knew that the chief priests
Had arrested Jesus out of fear and envy;
    But the chief priests stirred up the crowd,
    And urged them to ask for Barabbas.

539. (15:12-13)
So Pilate answered and said to them, again,
"Then what do you want me to do with Him
    Whom you call the King of the Jews?"
    And they shouted back, "Crucify him!"

540. (15:14)
Then Pilate said to them,
"Why? What evil has he done?"
    And they cried out even louder than before,
    "Crucify him!"

---

[136] This appears to be a nickname, meaning roughly "Daddy's Son."

541. (15:15)
And so Pilate, not wanting to provoke the crowd,
Gave Barabbas his freedom;
    And, after Jesus had been flogged,[137]
    Pilate turned Him over to be crucified.

The Soldiers Mock Jesus

542. (15:16)
Then…the soldiers led Jesus away[138]
And took Him to the courtyard
    Of the Governor's palace
    And called together all the guards on duty.

543. (15:17-18)
Then they dressed him in a purple robe,
Put a twisted crown of thorns on His head.
    And began to greet Him, by saying,
    "The BEST to you, King of the Jews!"

544. (15:19)
And they struck Him on the head, with a reed,
Over and over again, as they spit on Him,
    And kneeling before Him,
    They pretended to honor Him as king.

545. (15:20)
And after they had mocked Him,
They took off the purple robe;
    Dressed Him in His own clothes.
    And took Him away to be crucified.

---

[137] In the Roman system flogging was the first part of crucifixion, because flogging weakened the person and shortened the process of dying, although that was not compassion, it was so that the soldiers would not have an extra day of work.

[138] That is, away from where the trial had been h eld.

The Crucifixion of Jesus

546 (15:21)

As they left camp,[139] they met Simon of Cyrene,
The father of Alexander and Rufus,[140]
   He was coming in from the countryside.
   And they forced him to bear the crossbeam.[141]

547. (15:22-23)

So they took Jesus to a place, called "Golgotha,"[142]
Which means (in their language[143]), "Skull Place."[144]
   And they offered Him wine mixed with myrrh,
   But He refused it to drink it.

548. (15:24)

After they had crucified Him,[145]
They divided His garments,
   And cast lots for them,
   To find out what each man would take.

549. (15:25-26)

It was nine o'clock in the morning
When they crucified him.
   And the legal reason for execution was posted as:
   "THE KING OF THE JEWS."

---

[139] The place of execution was always outside the city gate,

[140] Alexander and Rufus, otherwise unknown in the New Testament, must have been prominent members in Rome.

[141] The medieval artists portrayed Jesus as carrying the whole cross (the two beams already joined together). But historical studies generally indicate a "tree" or vertical beam already in place at the place of execution and that the person condemned carried the cross beam.

[142] Pronunciation: GOAL-guh-thuh.

[143] That is, Aramaic

[144] And through Latin, we get "Calvary."

[145] Note: there is no description of the crucifixion, per se.

550. (15:27-28)
Two thieves were crucified with Jesus;
One at His right hand, and the other at His left.
    And the scripture was fulfilled, which says,
    "And He was treated like a criminal."

551. (15:29-30)
Those passing by scorn Him, wag their heads and say,
"Since You were going to destroy the temple,
    And build it back in three days,
    Come down from the cross and save yourself!

552. (15:31)
The chief priests and the scribes also mocked him
And said to each other,
    "He saved others,
    But He cannot save Himself.

553. (15:32)
"Let the Messiah, the King of Israel,
Come down from the cross,
    So that we may see and believe!"
    And even the ones crucified with him reviled Him.

ೞ ✿ ಐ

The Death of Jesus

554. (15:33-34a)
At noon darkness covered the entire area…

And it lasted till three o'clock in the afternoon'[146]
    That was when Jesus cried out with a loud voice,
    Saying, "Eloi, Eloi, Lama sabachthani?"

---

[146] This was a miraculous invention, because "An actual eclipse of the sun, of course, was impossible on Nisan 14, since the Passover occurred at the time of the full moon." (Paul L. Maier)

555. (15:34b-35)

This means, "My God, my God,
Why have you forsaken me?'[147]
    But, when some of those present heard it,
    They said, "Listen! He is calling for Elijah."[148]

556. (15:36)

And one of them ran and filled a sponge with vinegar,
Put it on a reed, and gave it to Jesus to drink,
    Saying, 'Hey! Wait and let us see
    If Elijah comes to take Him down!'

557. (15:37-38)

Then as Jesus heaved a loud sigh,
He breathed His last breath.
    And the veil of the temple was split open
    From the top to the bottom.[149]

ಸಾ ❦ ಲ

The Centurion

558. (15:39)

And the centurion, in charge of the crucifixion,
Was standing nearby and looking at Jesus,
    And when he sees Jesus take His last breath,
    He says, "This man was truly God's Son."

---

[147] These words are the opening words of Psalm 22, which depict the sufferings of Messiah, but with two differences: (1) ""my God" is given in Aramaic and (2) the verb, "forsake, leave, abandon" is a synonym for the Hebrew word used in the Bible.

[148] Probably, the Roman soldiers, who spoke Latin and Greek.

[149] Robert L. Plummer, "Something Awry in the Temple? The Rending of the Temple Veil and Early Jewish Sources that Report Unusual Phenomena in the Temple around A.D. 30. (The Evangelical Theological Society (https://www/etsjets. org >48-2-pp301-316 JETS; see also "Strange Happenings in the Temple."

The Women
559. (15:40)
Some women were there, also, watching at a distance.
Among these were Mary Magdalene, [150]and Mary,
   The mother of James the younger and of Joseph, [151]
   Along with Salome.

560. (15:41)
While Jesus did ministry in Galilee,
They, along with many other women,
   Who had gone to Jerusalem with Jesus,
   Had followed Him and prepared food for Him.

The Burial of Jesus
561. (15:42-43a)
It was late Friday afternoon,[152]
And the Sabbath was approaching,
   When Joseph arrived…
   From Arimathaea[153]

---

[150] Appendix 100 of *The Companion Bible* identifies the "The Six Marys," but when used of the Lord's mother (Matthew 1:16, etc.)., the name is always "Mariam" in Greek or Miriam" Hebrew "as in Exodus 15:20. The context leaves no doubt as to her identity. The other five are usually "Maria."

1. Mary the mother of James the less and Joses (Matthew 27:56. Mark 15:40; 16:1. Luke 24:10) is called "the other Mary" (Matthew 27:61; 28:1), and the wife of Cleopas (John 19:25).
2. Mary the sister of Martha, who anointed the Lord's feet (John 12:3), see Appendix 156 and Appendix 158. She is mentioned by name only in Luke 10:39, 42 and John 11:1, 2, 19, 20, 28, 31, 32, 45; and 12:3.
3. Mary Magdalene, (or Mary of Magdala, Matthew 15:39). She is always to be identified by this designation (Matthew 27:56. Mark 16:1, 9. Luke 8:2. John 20:18, etc.); there is no authority whatever for identifying her with the unnamed woman of Luke 7:37-50.
4. Mary the mother of John Mark (Acts 12:12).
5. Mary, one of Paul's helpers (Romans 16:6).

[151] Greek: Joses, a shortened for of Joseph.

[152] Or: the day of preparation.

[153] Pronunciation: Air-ri-muh-THAI-a-.

562. (15:43b)
He was an influential Law-Maker[154]
And one who longed eagerly for God's Kingdom.
    And even more, Joseph had the courage
      To go to Pilate and to ask for the body of Jesus.

563. (15:44)
And Pilate was surprised to hear,
That Jesus had died so quickly;
    So, in order to confirm His death,
    Pilate sent for the centurion.

564. (15:45b-46a)
And it was only then
That he gave the care of the body to Joseph,
    Who went and bought
    A piece of fine linen cloth.

565. (15:46b)
Then he removed the body from the cross,
And wrapped it in the linen cloth,
    And laid it in a tomb,
    That was hewn out of the rock.

566. (15:46c-47)
Then he rolled a large stone into place
To cover the opening of the tomb;
    And Mary Magdalene and Mary, the mother of Joey,
    Saw where Joseph placed the body.

---

[154] I have used "Law-Maker" for the Greek word that is generally translated as "Counselor" and was used to refer to a member of the Great Sanhedrin, which had seventy-one (71) members. It was both legislative and judicial. And under the liberal policy of Rome, it dealt with internal affairs, up to the death sentence. That was reserved for the Roman administration under the Governor, which, in Judea, from 26 to 36 AD, was Pontius Pilate.

Day Seven of Holy Week
(Saturday, Nisan 15)

The Body of Jesus Was in the Tomb

</////>

Note:
On the Fish
As a Symbol of the Faith
By the Translator

The Greek word for 'fish is "ichthus" (ΙΧΘΥΣ) (pronounced: IK-thous). Each letter can be seen as the initial letter of each of the following words "Jesus Christ (or Messiah), God's Son, Savior' which can then be read as:
    (1) 'Jesus (is) the Messiah, God's Son and (our) Savior' or
    (2) 'Jesus, the Messiah, (is) God's Son and (our) Savior' or
    (3) 'Jesus, the Messiah (and) God's Son (is our) Savior.

The Resurrection of Jesus confirms the truth that Jesus is the Messiah, God's Son, and our Savior! And when we accept Jesus as God's anointed Son and our Savior, we are made a New Creation and that is a true witness to Jesus as God's Messiah and Son.

Hallelujah! Praise the Lord!

CHAPTER 16

Day One of The New Creation
(Sunday, Nisan 16)

The Resurrection

Three Women Receive the Message: "He is risen!"

567. (16:1)
When the Sabbath had ended,[155]
Mary Magdalene, Mary, the mother of James,[156]
   And Salome, went and bought some sweet spices
   So that they could go and anoint Him.

568. (16:2)
Then very early in the morning,
Of Day One[157] of the new week,
   They were on their way to the tomb
   As the sun was rising.

---

[155] After sunset on Saturday

[156] Mary Magdalene was an organized person, who stayed on the top of thigs. Mary, mother of James, must be the mother of Jesus. She, above all, was interested in her Son. ❖ In the Jewish culture of the first century, a female was identified by the closest, living male in the kinship circle: (1) first, as daughter of her father, (2) then, as the wife of her husband, and (3) and the mother of her oldest, living son, then the next, etc. At that time James, the brother of Jesus, was the head pastor in Jerusalem. He was martyred in A.D. 62. Apparently, this was written no later than A.D. 62.

[157] Greek: "Day One" which reflects the terminology in Genesis 1.

569. (16:3-4)
But the only thing they could think about was:
"Who is going to move that big stone for us?"
    But, when they got closer and looked up again,
    They saw that the stone was no longer there.

570. (16:5)
And when they entered the tomb,
They saw a young man sitting on the right side,
    He was wearing a long, white robe;
    And they were absolutely amazed.

571. (16:6)
And he says to them, "Do not be paralyzed with fear!
I know that you are looking for Jesus of Nazareth!
    The One who was crucified! But He is risen!
    He is not here! Come see where they laid Him."

572. (16:7)
"Now, go tell His disciples…"and Peter,"
That He is going before you into Galilee,
    Just as He told you,
    And you shall see Him, there!"

573. (16:8)
So they left abruptly
And ran away from the tomb,
    Because they were horrified
    And trembling with fear.

574. (16:9)

And, they were so overcome
With panic and terror,[158]
    That they did not stop
    Nor say a word to anyone.

ಏ ✿ ಌ

Three Appearances of Jesus

-o0o-

(1) To Mary Magdalene

575. (16:9)

After Jesus had risen from the dead,
Early on the first day of the week,
    He first appeared to Mary Magdalene
    Out of whom He had cast seven demons.

---

[158] There is a glaring disjuncture between verse 8 and what follows. This is one of many, abrupt "gaps" in the Gospel of Mark. One can imagine that Mary Magdalene, either on the way to her quarters or after she arrived there, realized, "this fear and terror is not what Jesus taught; I must face up to this. So I will go back to the tomb and face it." The account here is also related in Luke and John. Most scholars today affirm that the last twelve verses are not original to Mark and while there are manuscripts that have the long addition, others with a short addition end with verse 8. I will speak to this problem from two points of view: (1) As a biblical scholar and ((2) as a Charismatic, Pentecostal, who has seen people healed and demons cast out. What is objectionable in the last twelve verses is the section in "Signs Following." If the last twelve verses had not been original, no one could have inserted the later due to the Signs following section. And, because of this passage, later scribes separated it from the body of the Gospel. Counting manuscripts is of little help because they reflect latter opinions and do not come from the first generation of writers.

576. (16:10-11)
And she went and told the good news to His followers,
While they were grieving and weeping.
   But when they heard that Jesus was alive,
   And had been seen by her, they did not believe it.

-o0o-

(2) To Two Disciples

577. (16:12-13)
Later, Jesus appeared to two of them, *incognito*,[159]
As they were walking along, leaving the city.
   And they came back and told it to the others:
   But they did not even believe them.

-o0o-

(3) To the Eleven

578. (16:14)
Later Jesus appeared to the eleven, themselves,
As they were eating together.
   And He rebuked them for their unbelief
   And the hardness of their hearts.

579. (16:14)
And He said this
Because they had not believed
   Those who had seen Him
   After He had risen.

---

[159] Greek: "In another form."

80. (16:15)

He also said to them,
"Go everywhere,[160] in the inhabited earth,
    And proclaim the Good-News[161] of salvation
    To every human being.[162]

581. (16:16)

Whoever believes[163] and is baptized
Shall be saved;
    But whoever does not believe
    Shall be condemned.

ಸಿ ✿ ಣ

Signs Following

582. (16:17)

And these are the signs that God will send
To confirm the ministry of those who believe.
    In my name they shall cast out demons;
    And they shall speak with new tongues.

583. (16:18)

They will also take up serpents with their hands;
And if they drink poison, it shall not hurt them;
    They shall lay hands on the sick,
    And they shall be healed.

---

[160] "Going (or as you go) into all the world" is the literal translation of the Greek text, but a parallel construction in Hebrew is also used as an imperative; therefore the King James, "Go ye therefore…"

[161] Or "preach the Gospel."

[162] Greek: "All creation" or "Every creature." This reminds us that all creation suffers because of sin and "groans" as it awaits that glorious redemption.

[163] 'To believe' means "to turn from sin and to turn to God or to surrender our lives to God."

☙ ❀ ❧
Jesus Ascends and…
584.(16:19)
So then, the Lord Jesus, for His part,
After He had spoken with them,
>   Was taken up into heaven,
>   And He sat down at the right hand of God

.

☙ ❀ ❧
His Disciples Go on Mission
585. (16:20
And His disciples, for their part,
Went forth and preached everywhere,
>   As the Lord worked with them;
>   And confirmed the Word with signs and miracles.

Amen!

About the Author and Translator

James M. Beaty was born in 1925 in Johnston County, North Carolina, where came to Christian faith and was baptized in the Holy Spirit in 1940. He attended Atlantic Christian College (now Barton College), in Wilson, North Carolina, graduating in 1945, then majored in Systematic Theology at Vanderbilt University School of Religion, graduating with a B.D. in 1949, before pursuing his Ph.D. from Vanderbilt in Biblical Studies with a minor in Reformation and completing that degree in 1963.

Before pursuing a teaching career in the United States, Beaty spent sixteen years under appointment by Church of God World Missions in Haiti, the Dominican Republic, and Chile, where he established and headed biblical training programs. Returning from South America, he taught at Lee College from 967 until 1974. He then established and headed a Spanish-speaking ministerial training school in Houston, Texas, from 1975 to 1980. Following that, Beatty served as Academic Dean of the Church of God School of Theology (now Pentecostal Theological Seminary), for twelve years, while he continued teaching half-time until he retired in 2001. The long-time Society for Pentecostal Studies member became Executive Secretary of the organization in 1972 and President in 1975.

Dr. Beaty is highly esteemed among Pentecostal Bible scholars, theologians, and Church persons. As this work goes to press, he turned ninety-nine in January 2024 and is counting down to one hundred.

www.ingramcontent.com/pod-product-compliance
Lightning Source LLC
Chambersburg PA
CBHW070101080526
44586CB00013B/1150